TODAY'S THOUGHT

*Rev. Paul S. Osumi:
the Man and His Message*

TODAY'S THOUGHT

*Rev. Paul S. Osumi:
the Man and His Message*

Norman H. Osumi

LEGACY ISLE
PUBLISHING

© 2013 Norman H. Osumi

All rights reserved. No part of this book may be reproduced in any form or by any electronic or mechanical means, including information retrieval systems, without prior written permission from the publisher, except for brief passages quoted in reviews.

ISBN 978-1-935690-41-2

Library of Congress Control Number: 2013945828

Design and production
Angela Wu-Ki

Legacy Isle Publishing
1000 Bishop St., Suite 806
Honolulu, Hawai'i 96813
www.legacyislepubishing.net
info@legacyislepublishing.net

Printed in the United States

To my father, Rev. Paul S. Osumi, who helped countless people, many of whom were not known to him, but only to God

CONTENTS

1	Foreword	
6	Acknowledgments	
8	Introduction	

13   PART ONE
     Biography

15	Chapter 1	*From Japan through College*
28	Chapter 2	*From Marriage through Early Ministries in Hilo and on Kauaʻi*
39	Chapter 3	*Arrest After Pearl Harbor*
48	Chapter 4	*Sand Island Detention Camp and Lordsburg Internment Camp, New Mexico*
57	Chapter 5	*Released to Gila Relocation Camp*
77	Chapter 6	*Return to Hawaiʻi*
95	Chapter 7	*Today's Thought*
97	Chapter 8	*Last Years of Life*

103 PART TWO
     Inspirational Messages

106 Hilo Japanese Christian Church (1936 – 1938)
     Living Creatively
     The Mystery of Life
     Finding Ourselves
     The Imperishable Hope

119	Lihue Christian Church (1938 – 1941)
	Sympathy
	The Nurture of the Soul
	Living Without Complaint
	The Eyes of the Heart
129	Canal Church—Gila Relocation Camp (1943 – 1945)
	Is Life Worth Living?
	Spirit of Adventure
	Being on Top of the World
	The Secrets of Not Losing Heart
137	Waialua Pilgrim Church (1946 – 1949)
	What is Your Average?
	Making the Most of Ordinary Abilities
	On Being Fully Alive
	Secrets of Married Happiness
159	ʻEwa Community Church (1949 – 1958)
	Living Peaceably with Others
	Are You Impatient?
	How Are Your Nerves?
	No Man is an Island
184	Nuʻuanu Congregational Church (1958 – 1980)
	Things That Money Cannot Buy
	Remember Who You Are
	God in the Desert
	Your Style of Life
195	PART THREE
	Today's Thought

Resolutions for a Happy Life

No one will ever get out of this world alive. Therefore...

Resolve to maintain a reasonable sense of values.
Take care of yourself. Good health is everyone's major source of wealth. Without it, happiness is harder to attain and sometimes almost impossible.

Resolve to be cheerful and helpful.
People will repay you in kind. Avoid angry, abrasive people. They are generally vengeful. Avoid zealots (fanatics, cranks, loners). They are generally humorless.

Resolve to listen more and talk less.
No one ever learns anything by talking. Be chary (cautious) of giving advice. Wise men do not need it and fools will not heed it.

Resolve to be tender with the young, compassionate with the aged, sympathetic with the striving, and tolerant of the weak and the wrong.
Sometimes in life, you will be all of these. Do not equate money with success. There are many successful moneymakers who are miserable failures as human beings. What counts most about success is how a person achieves it.

—Rev. Paul S. Osumi

FOREWORD

WHY I WROTE THIS BOOK

When I retired from the banking industry in 2003, I wanted to write a book featuring many of my father Paul S. Osumi's Today's Thoughts.

I had worked in the banking industry—at First Hawaiian Bank, Southeast Computer Associates (Liberty Bank and Bank of Honolulu), Bank of Hawai'i and Central Pacific Bank—for close to 40 years. For all those years I managed computer systems, and I wanted to do something different.

In today's world, so many people are looking for daily encouragement. Over the years, countless people told me that they read my father's daily inspirational thoughts in the newspaper. Beginning in 1957, he wrote and published these sayings for more than 35 years, first in the *Honolulu Advertiser* and then later in the *Hawaii Hochi* and the *Fairbanks Daily News-Miner* in Alaska. Many people told me they cut his sayings out of the newspaper and kept the clippings in their wallets, at work and at home.

I thought writing a book that includes my father's Today's Thoughts would give people encouragement and guidance in their daily living. Mr. Denis Isono, my last manager at Central Pacific Bank, kept asking me if my book was finished, as this project was one of the reasons I retired from Central Pacific Bank.

In 2002, a local publishing company reprinted three volumes of my father's Today's Thoughts and distributed them in bookstores throughout Hawai'i. After I retired, though, I noticed the books were not being promoted in the stores and sales had declined. I was able to buy the remaining inventory from the publishing company.

In November 2006, my wife and I advertised and sold the three volumes as a set, offering them through mail order, Logos Bookstore and Nuʻuanu Congregational Church. To our surprise, we sold 1,600 sets of books in one month— almost our entire inventory. People who wrote or spoke to me during this time encouraged me to write more books featuring my father's daily sayings. When we depleted our inventory of Volume II, we discontinued selling the sets since we were not planning to reprint any of the books.

The experience convinced me that I should publish additional books that included Father's daily sayings. I planned to categorize the sayings by subject: marriage, family, health, work, retirement, wealth, faith and death. I started thinking about how to gather all this information, since the daily sayings were unorganized. Some were typed, others were handwritten and still others were newspaper clippings.

Around this time, I met people at the Japanese Cultural Center of Hawaiʻi (JCCH). After my mother passed away in August 2003 (Father had passed away seven years before), we donated many of the Japanese items my parents had received and collected over the years to the JCCH. I met the JCCH gift shop manager, Barbara Ishida, and talked to her about the items. I mentioned that I was uncertain what to do with the many boxes containing letters, documents, photographs, sermons and my father's daily sayings. I was ready to discard them.

Ms. Ishida quickly introduced me to then-JCCH President Judge Riki May Amano and to Jane Kurahara, who was the JCCH manager and resource center volunteer. They explained that Father's collection of documents would be a welcome addition to their resource center. The files would be preserved and catalogued in their archives for future reference. Can you imagine? I almost threw away all of my father's files!

To assist in the archiving process, I volunteered to catalog Father's documents. I started reading his journals, as well as letters he wrote and received from my mother, military authorities, Christian leaders, friends and church members. The more I read, the more interested I became in my father's past, which he rarely talked about. He almost never mentioned the war years, when he was interned and encountered many disappointments and much hardship and disgrace. Many people told me it was common for the older generation, especially fathers, not to tell their children about their lives.

    I began researching his life, which took me to his high school alma mater, now Mid-Pacific Institute, and to the University of Hawai'i, where he graduated in 1930 with a Bachelor of Arts and Sciences degree. I pored over military archives, visited the Japanese Consulate of Honolulu and traveled to the neighbor islands and mainland. I consulted newspaper articles and local books that referenced him. I gathered information from people who knew him, and wrote down family recollections of things we did and stories related to us by our parents while we were growing up.

    During this process of researching and writing, which I started more than 10 years ago, I faced many difficulties. First, I struggled with writing about my father as I uncovered information about the war years. I thought about his hardship and could not understand why the United States government interned him.

    My feelings about the government were mixed. Sometimes I understood, but at other times I felt anger. However, I did not want to interject my personal feelings into the book and continued to try to look at the past as straight history.

    Second, I kept trying to put myself in his shoes, and to write the book the way he would have written it. I believe he would be happy that I am including a few of his sermons and a selection from Today's Thought.

    There was so much information, I wasn't sure what to include and what to leave out. I wondered whether there would be interest in the book. There were many distractions; friends told me that I should dedicate time each day to writing or I would never get the book done. With age, my eyes were making reading and writing more difficult. Finally, I did not type very well, so secretaries typed everything for me while I was working. (What an excuse!)

Whenever I talked to people about writing this book, they asked, "When will the book be available?" Over the years, the writing of this book took me in different directions and it got much more complex and difficult than I'd anticipated. Then in 2012, through the JCCH, I met Gail Honda, who would become my editor and provide me with the direction and enthusiasm to finish. She helped me decide what to include and exclude in the book, and helped shape and edit its contents.

This book, then, is the fruit of my labor. Using the research and information I collected, I, as his youngest son, provide here my personal feelings and insights on the man that was Reverend Paul S. Osumi. This book covers his life, accomplishments, faith, ministry, wisdom and hardships. I also, as his son, explain how I believe he arrived at the inspirational messages he passed on during his lifetime.

Growing up, I saw him as a father and grandfather first and not as a minister. My wife and children say the same thing. In this book are things he said to me that I still hold to be true for a happy life today. During my years in the banking industry, I believe his influence guided me as an employee and as a manager.

I dedicate this book to my father in hopes that people who read it will come to know, "Who was Reverend Paul S. Osumi?" I hope you will gain some of his wisdom through his inspirational thoughts.

The first part of this book is devoted to his life. It tells how Father came to be the person who wrote all of the Today's Thought columns. The latter part of this book includes excerpts from his sermons, and selected inspirational sayings from Today's Thought. The sermons started in the 1930s and Today's Thought dates from 1957. My father was a Protestant minister, but his Today's Thought columns were read by people of all religions. It did not matter who you were or what church you attended; hundreds of letters that people wrote to my father over the years show me the diversity of his audience.

People warned me that if I waited too long, everyone who knew Father would be gone. I believe this may be true, since the younger generation will not know him by name. Others told me that what he wrote is timeless and that the younger generation will learn things from his inspirational sayings.

It is in this light that I hope this book will give you, the reader, inspiration and guidance in living a happy and meaningful life.

ACKNOWLEDGMENTS

This book has taken many years to complete. The following people gave me the encouragement, support, assistance and information to complete the book. I believe that without them, it would not have been written.

My wife, Carolyn, provided me the encouragement and support from the beginning to see this project to completion. We traveled together to the mainland and Neighbor Islands, meeting with many people who played a part in my father's life. She also made a number of suggestions that I incorporated into this book.

Dr. Gail Honda provided direction and guidance in the organization and content of the book and served as its editor. She recommended that I present my father's biography from a son's perspective on what may have influenced both the writing of Today's Thought and my own life. Dr. Honda took the large amount of data representing many years of research that I had gathered for my father's biography and edited it to a size that made this book interesting and enjoyable to read.

Yoshiko Yanagawa, Nobue Uchida and Dorothy Harada, the three daughters of Mr. and Mrs. Sakujiro Yuki, contributed their knowledge and information about my parents when we were in Arizona's Gila Relocation Camp during the war years. They generously gave of their time to meet or write to me about camp events and living conditions, as well as my father's life challenges. Father was very blessed to have this family so close to him in the relocation camp. Personally, I cannot ever thank this family enough for what they have given to my family.

Jane Kurahara, a JCCH Resource Center staff associate, encouraged me to write this book from the first day I met her at JCCH. She reminded me of the importance of our Japanese heritage in Hawai'i and of my father's own legacy in the Islands as part of this heritage. She has always been there to help and support me.

Betsy Young, who is also a JCCH Resource Center staff associate, provided continued support in gathering additional information and photos of my father over the years. She introduced me to Sanae Morita so that we could meet the Lihuʻe Christian Church members who knew my father on Kauaʻi prior to World War II. (Betsy had been a little girl attending that church when my father was the minister there.)

Sanae Morita, a member of the Lihuʻe Christian Church congregation, introduced me and my wife to other church members who remembered my parents. She helped schedule meetings with these people and continued to assist me in following up with them for further information.

Dr. Steve Takaki gave me many suggestions, recommendations, encouragement and information as I wrote this book over the years. His comments were instrumental in helping me complete the project. Each time I saw him, he would ask, "How is the book coming along?" I sincerely appreciate all the things Dr. Takaki has done for me.

Linda Quarberg generously gave of her time to type some of my father's sermons. Using all of his notes and comments in the outlines, she did excellent work in interpreting and formatting the sermons into readable form. She also provided guidance in getting this book published.

Christy Takamune, the JCCH Gallery/Gift Shop manager, also helped refer me to people who would assist me in publishing this book.

Michelle Miyashiro, JCCH's administrative assistant, offered additional support at that organization, including helping me reach the right people there.

Dorothy Kusumoto provided her time and support in doing the final editing of my father's sermons.

There were so many other people I met over the years who gave me encouragement to do this book. Even if I have failed to recognize you here, please accept my sincere appreciation and gratitude.

INTRODUCTION

Three excerpts epitomize Rev. Paul Osumi's contributions to both Japanese-American and Hawai'i's culture.

Rev. Grant S. C. Lee wrote:

I remember the Rev. Paul Osumi as a pastor who was a "people" person, wanting for people to be in right relationships with one another and with God. He knew that people inherently longed to be in nurturing, loving and growing relationships for and with one another. He nurtured this by offering practical life-principles through his writings as well as through his sermons. I believe this is the reason why his "Today's Thoughts" ran so long in the dailies and was so popularly read.

His sermons were the same way, driven by a passion for people to practice the art of nurturing right relationships in everyday living for the sake of inner peace as well as for global, communal peace. I remember a poignant sermon he preached on Jesus' Beatitudes. He said, if one read the Beatitudes (Matthew 5:1-12) once a day for a whole year, the outcome would be a deeper understanding of the relational, peace-living quality of life seen through the eyes of Christ.

The Rev. Paul S. Osumi was my personal mentor who taught me that valuing and practicing right relationships inclusively, with all people, without prejudice, was the central core of ministry.

In his ministry, the Rev. Osumi was a visionary. He was a pastor who was ahead of the times. He taught a faith which looked outwards towards the formation of a world moved by peace and justice for all humankind. Even though he was subjected to injustice through his stay at the Gila River Relocation Camp, he held no animosity. He humbly ministered for the sake of the common good in the community of the disenfranchised.

As an Asian-American, he chose to study for the Christian ministry in a graduate school of religion made up of mostly dominant-culture students. Through these challenging experiences, he was able to engage in a meaningful, wisdom-filled, peace-giving ministry which positively touched many lives in the process of life's long journey.

In looking at ministry to and with youth, he valued them as contributing members of the church and society in the "here-and-now," and not simply for the future. His strong conviction was seeing youth as deliverers of peace who had the capacities to create a new peace-giving, peace-living world. Thus, he advocated for a strong and vital youth ministry program in the church where we both served.

With a heart full of gratitude for the life and ministry of the Rev. Paul S. Osumi, I humbly submit this brief narrative in memory of the one who was a spiritual mentor to many!

The Toastmasters International District 49 honored him, as well:

The Rev. Paul Osumi may be the best-read author in Hawaii. For more than 37 years, Osumi has written a short, inspirational column called "Today's Thought" for the Honolulu Advertiser. "In the beginning, eight ministers from different faiths were asked to contribute," he recalls. "I outlasted them all because I didn't write about my own theology, I wrote about real life."

His urge to continue to collect and to write is fueled by the tremendous support and encouragement from thousands of readers. In letters, telephone calls and comments from chance meetings—therein lie the inspiration and motivation to carry on. For example, one reader wrote: "One of your articles saved our marriage." An AIDS patient had this to say: "Your 'Today's Thought' gives me hope in my life and courage to go on." Still another letter added: "You have helped me more than you will know."

Osumi ended up in an internment camp in the New Mexico desert. "The camp was the best time in my life," he says, even though the conditions made him dangerously ill. "I got the opportunity to minister to the people who were desperate. Even getting sick taught me how to be a better minister.

"I do it to remind busy people to look for meaning in their lives. Life without meaning is really nothing."

And Greg Wiles, a *Honolulu Advertiser* staff writer, wrote:

Among pages full of bad news and grief, The Rev. Paul Osumi's column, Today's Thoughts, was a tightly written chestnut providing people with simple hope, wisdom and optimism.

"Today's Thoughts" can be found taped to walls, placed on desks and folded up in wallets across the state and on the Mainland. For more than 38 years his column touched people with simple ideas aimed to inspire and provide insight.

This was the message he selected for the next day for the Advertiser readers: "Life is a day —this day. All past days are gone beyond reviving. All days that still may come for you or me are veiled in the great mystery and there may not be another for either of us. Therefore this day is Life, and life begins anew with it. However discouraging your days may have been thus far, keep this thought in your mind—Life begins each morning."

"Life is 90 percent attitude," Osumi said once in an Advertiser interview. "The kind of attitude you have determines the kind of life you're going to live."

People half-jokingly said he had the largest congregation of any minister in the state and that he was Hawaii's best-read author. President and Mrs. Reagan once wrote to him saying how much they enjoyed one of the three collections of "Today's Thoughts" that Osumi published.

The Reagans received the book from the late U.S. Senator Sparky Matsunaga, also a fan. Others who offered praise of the ministry's writing were U.S. Vice President Hubert Humphrey, industrial mogul Henry Kaiser, and conductor Andre Kostelanetz.

Hawaii Hochi Publisher Paul Yempuku remembers that Osumi's messages also found a following with readers of his Japanese-language newspaper. "Once in a while a customer used to call me and say the first thing they read is not the front page, but his column," he recalled. ❦

Part One

BIOGRAPHY

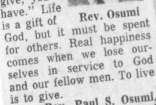

Today's Thought

If all we do is done for ourselves, our lives lose their beauty and meaning. At the heart of life there seems to be a law that says, "What you keep, you lose; and what you give, you have." Life is a gift of God, but it must be spent for others. Real happiness comes when we lose ourselves in service to God and our fellow men. To live is to give.
—Rev. Paul S. Osumi, Nuuanu Congregational Church.

Rev. Osumi

Today's Thought

Music can bring enlargement of mind and heart. It uplifts us and carries us out of ourselves. It brings our souls out of the narrow confines of routine. It transports us from our mundane world to an enchanged world of beautiful sounds. It behooves all of us to cultivate good music and enrich our starving souls.
—Rev. Paul S. Osumi, Nuuanu Congregational Church.

Rev. Osumi

CHAPTER 1

From Japan through College

My father did not talk about his parents, nor his childhood in Japan, while I was growing up. I have a few pictures of my father's parents, but I did not know them because they lived in Japan during my lifetime. According to my mother, my father's parents had come to Hawaiʻi before he was born. His mother returned to Japan while pregnant with him, and he was born there. His father also returned to Japan, and I don't believe my grandparents visited Hawaiʻi again after I was born.

Father was born on June 15, 1905 in Kusatsu, Hiroshima, the second son and eighth child of Usaburo and Yoshi Osumi. His mother named him Sutekichi, which means "Throwaway," because she did not want him. I do not know how that name affected his life, but it must have had a psychological impact on him.

According to Japanese Consulate records, Usaburo came alone to Hawaiʻi on January 31, 1913, eight years after my father was born. Records do not show Usaburo and Yoshi in Hawaiʻi before 1913, although my mother said they were.

According to Father's passport, on September 12, 1919, when he was 14, he left Japan and arrived in Honolulu, Territory of Hawaiʻi. It must have been frightening for him to travel on the ship by himself, not speaking any English. It is unclear why his mother sent him to Hawaiʻi, except that she did not want him and was sending him to live with his father.

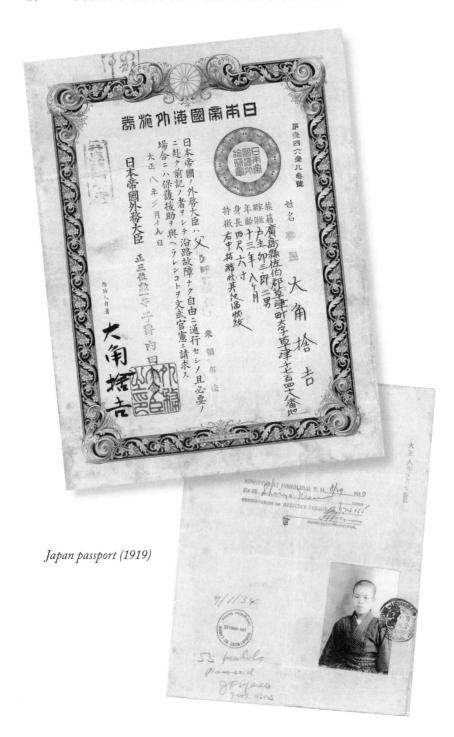

Japan passport (1919)

10th Avenue home in Kaimuki, Hawaii

My father lived with his father, who was a cook at Fort Shafter, on 10th Avenue in the Kaimuki area of Honolulu. According to Japanese Consulate records, Usaburo returned to Japan on April 20, 1920, after my father had lived with him for only seven months. Why his father returned to Japan, leaving him in Hawai'i, I do not know. My father never saw his parents again.

After Usaburo returned to Japan, my father stayed with his older brother, Torakichi. Torakichi owned a Japanese restaurant called Fukujutei, which was located behind the Toyo Theater and next to the Kokusai Theater near A'ala Park. I have been told that the restaurant was famous for its shrimp tempura. According to my mother, my father said he worked very hard at the restaurant and yet his brother and the brother's wife scolded him. He lived above the restaurant for about five months before enrolling at Mills Institute for Boys (now Mid-Pacific Institute), which was then a boarding school. At some point, one of his sisters came to Hawai'i and lived in Hilo, while the rest of his family stayed in Japan.

Mills Institute for Boys (1920)

Grammar and High School

June Yahiku, of the Mid-Pacific Institute (MPI) Office of Advancement, helped me learn about my father's early schooling through his records, which were in the school's archives. Father attended Trinity Mission School, an Episcopal school, through fourth grade. In September 1920, he transferred to Mills Institute for Boys (the girls' school was called Kawaiahaʻo Seminary) entering as a sixth grader (he skipped fifth grade). He graduated from high school in 1926.

According to MPI's archives, he earned mostly As and a few Bs, which qualified him for the Scholarship Honor Roll program during all four years. The school year was divided into six terms, each six weeks long. Grades were distributed at the end of each term, and those who earned an A in more than half of their subjects were put on the Scholarship Honor Roll program. This was the first time I knew about my father's academic achievements; he never spoke about them to me. I felt very proud of him. I began to appreciate the hardships he must have faced growing up, not wanted by his parents and living on his own.

In 1922, when he was a ninth grader, tuition was $150 for grammar school and $175 for high school. His older brother may have helped pay for some of his tuition and/or expenses. Other portions of his tuition were paid by being an honor-roll student and through work scholarships. He earned $75 in his sophomore year by working at the swimming pool, and during his junior year he earned $125 working in the laundry room. An article I discovered stated, "An explosion took place in the laundry. Paul Osumi, who was working there, was injured and taken to the hospital. It was learned by authorities that a leakage in the gas pipe was the cause of the explosion." He had never mentioned this incident to me.

Further research in MPI's archives made me realize that it was at school that my father was first influenced by Christian values. One document described MPI as a Christian boarding school (I understand it had boarders until about the 1980s) that had, as its aim, to develop:

...sound Christian character and high ideals of citizenship among its students. Interracial friendship and sympathy are promoted in all the school activities and represent one of its finest features. Mid-Pacific Institute is a product of the missionary spirit and influence in Hawaii. It emphasizes the religious side of life and brings every helpful means to bear upon its students in the develop-

Paul Osumi as a student

WINS ESSAY PRIZE

Paul Osumi, Mid-Pacific Institute senior, who shares first prize in the Friend Peace Scholarship contest with K. Inouye of Lahainaluna high schol, Maui. He will will go to the University of Hawaii.

ESSAY PRIZE WON BY POPULAR BOY

Osumi Is Track Captain and Holds Important Class Offices

Paul Osumi, senior in the Mid-Pacific Institute high school, tied with K. Inouye of Lahainaluna high school for first honors in the Friend Peace Scholarship contest. These two young men rendered such splendid essays that the judges divided the first and second prizes between them. Each will receive $800, or $200 annually.

Paul Osumi is the second Mid-Pacific student to receive this award. Last year Samuel Kawahara won second place with a scholarship of $150 annually.

Osumi is a popular student at Mid-Pacific, holding many important offices as well as taking part in school activities. He was a member of the Mid-Pacific debating team that captured first honors in the interscholastic debate for the governor's trophy and also vice president of the senior class, Damon Lyceum society and Mills C. E. society. He is also a member of the Hi-Y club and the glee club. He is also a talented track artist and was four years captain of his class track team, breaking the Waipahu-Mills relay record this year. He was for three years member of the Mills four mile relay team, besides being on the swimming team.

Osumi plans to enter the University of Hawaii next fall. His scholastic standing is third in his class with an average of 95 per cent in his four years of high school work.

Newspaper article (1926)

ment of strong Christian character. Daily chapel services are held and students are required to attend the church and Sunday school of their choice. The boys and girls maintain religious organizations of their own. Mid-Pacific Institute emphasizes the necessity and dignity of honest, useful work.

During his high school years, my father showed signs of being an excellent writer and speaker, and this would later help him to develop and deliver sermons during his ministries. He was associate editor for *Ke Anuenue*, the school paper, and tied for first place in the Friend Peace Scholarship essay contest. This was a contest, open to Japanese boys, with the goal of establishing good relations between the United States and Japan. The essay's subject was: "After Exclusion, What?" Prizes were: First place, $1,000; second place, $600; and third place, $300.

Father tied with a Lahainaluna High School student for first honors. His essay was titled, "How to Keep Peace in the Pacific." He received $800 (the first and second place prizes were added together and divided by two), or $200 annually to help pay for his tuition at the University of Hawai'i for four years. Regrettably, I could not locate a copy of his essay.

From an early age, my father was recognized as an outstanding orator. While in grammar school, he took first place honors in the declamation contest, in which contestants were judged on their pronunciation, enunciation, presentation, preparation and interpretation. For that contest, he delivered Lincoln's "Gettysburg Address." I knew he held President Lincoln in high regard, since he had a picture of the President in his home office for many years. In the eighth grade, he won the Silver Cup for first place in the Damon Lyceum Oratorical Contest, and he was a member of the debate team that captured first honors in the interscholastic debate for the Governor's trophy.

Father was active in clubs and student government and took on numerous leadership roles, such as vice president, treasurer and secretary of the Damon Lyceum Society, which helped plan the school's annual socials; vice president of the Mills Christian Endeavor Society; vice president and secretary of the Literary Societies; and he was a member of the HI-Y Club and Glee Club. On February 21, 1925, when a joint meeting between Mills, the boys' school, and Kawaiaha'o, the girls' school, took place for the first time, he spoke on "The Task Before Us" and was described as a "leader."

In addition to receiving accolades for his written and oratorical achievements, my father was also an excellent athlete, notably as a runner. In the eighth grade, he started a 17-mile relay run with nine other boys. The eighth graders won that year, and he had the best time on the team. In a solo one-mile run, he came in third. By ninth grade, he was running the 17-mile relay as its anchor runner. In his senior year as a marathon runner, he won a Silver Cup for first place in cross-country running and was referred to as the "mainstay" of the cross-country team. As captain of the track team in his final four years, he helped break the Waipahu-Mills relay record.

Father did mention to me that he was a long-distance runner in high school, but he never told me how far he ran or about the awards he received.

It was also documented that he was on the swim team, but I found very little information about that.

When he graduated from Mills, his scholastic standing was third in his class. He had an average of 93 percent in his

Paul Osumi, senior year high school picture (1926)

four years of high school work, and was an honor roll student all four years. Because he came from Japan at the age of 14, and had to learn the English language at that age, I give my father tremendous credit for winning honors in essays and speeches.

He was described in the 1926 Mills yearbook. Next to his senior photo, it says:

The grand old man of the class, very solemn, but very scholarly. He carries a long face wherever he may be. He is a debater of great force and an orator of real worth. Because of these accomplishments he has served in many offices and has made good in all of them. But still he has a great weakness, and that is girls—he'd rather die than talk with one of the fair sex.

I was curious as to how he met my mother since he had this "weakness." In one of my father's sermons, he mentioned that he met my mother at a social gathering. I can only imagine how nervous he must have been, meeting her for the first time and talking to her.

Father mentioned to me that he was mischievous, and that he and his friends would sneak out of the dormitory at night to buy noodles when they were hungry. He also told me that he owned a racing car and would race up and down the old, winding Nuʻuanu Pali road. He never discouraged me from owning Corvettes.

College Years

After graduating from Mills in 1926, my father attended and boarded at the University of Hawaiʻi (UH) at Mānoa.

At UH, he continued to be active in student life by serving as president of the Friend Peace Club. He was also a reporter for the student newspaper *Ka Leo o Hawaiʻi*; a member of the YMCA and Japanese Students Association Club, and recipient of a Theodore Richards Scholarship. Towards the end of his freshman year, he received a Certificate of Leadership from the Nuʻuanu YMCA. He had worked at the YMCA for two years in rural Oʻahu under Lloyd Killiam, visiting plantation camps during the summer months to conduct youth programs. This experience may have planted the seed for his ministry in later years, when he very much enjoyed working with children and youth groups.

In the summer before his senior year at UH, he worked on the island of Hawaiʻi at vacation summer schools around the Kohala area. From his diary, I was able to get a glimpse of his formative years working with youths. He wrote:

> *Our aim: To help boys and girls have a happy, healthy and helpful time, in the Christian way, at home, out-of-doors, at work, at play and in the church.*
>
> *Reminders:*
>
> 1. *Do nothing before a child which you do not wish the child to do.*
>
> 2. *Let nothing touch the senses of a child which you do not wish to become a permanent part of his life.*
>
> 3. *A teacher teaches a little by what he says, more by what he does, most by what he is.*
>
> 4. *A teacher teaches most and best when he secures the pupil's activity, when this activity is purposeful on the part of the child and requires his judgment and choice, and when this purposeful and thoughtful activity is cooperative.*

Most Effective Teaching:

To be actively in the background of an operation is the teacher's place. True control comes from within. It is individual. We need not teacher-dominated, but self-controlled boys and girls, working out problems, growing out of their own needs.

To help without hindering; to guide without directing; to bring forth and not put in; these summarize the progressive principles of methods in dealing with youth at work. True education is expression.

Docile Youths—Hope of Future:

Strong characters in the tomorrow of life depend on the strength of character developed today. Young hearts are easily turned to God and young minds readily learn to reason on problems of right and wrong.

Therefore, in your work of helping boys and girls think rightly you are helping to build fine characters for the future and are making sure of the world becoming a better place.

I am impressed by what he wrote in his diary; this may have started him thinking about helping and giving guidance to people in their daily lives.

Father received a Bachelor of Arts and Science degree from UH on June 2, 1930. Following graduation that summer, at age 25, he took a trip to Japan on the N.Y.K. ship *Asama Maru* and stayed there for two months under the auspices of UH, along with four other people: Masayuki Adachi, Luther Cox, Yoshinobu Sasaki and Herbert Wood. All had either just graduated, like my father, or were former UH graduates. They were entertained by the *Asahi Shinbum*, Tokyo's leading daily newspaper at the time, and Kibosha, a cultural organization whose members came from all over Japan. I do not know how he was selected by UH, but it must have been an honor.

"U" Excursion Sails For Japan

Left to right: Yoshinobu Sasaki, Herbert Wood, Luther Cox, Masayuki Adachi and Paul Osumi.

FIVE YOUNG MEN TO SEE ORIENT

Two Get Teaching Positions in East; Three Returning

Five young men, traveling under the name of the University of Hawaii excursion party, are leaving on a two-month tour of Japan on board the N. Y. K. motorship Asama Maru this afternoon. The group includes Masayuki Adachi, Luther Cox, Paul Osumi, Yoshinobu Sasaki and Herbert Wood.

While in Japan, the young men, who are all either graduates or former students of the University of Hawaii, will be entertained by the Tokyo Asahi Shimbun, leading daily newspaper of Tokyo, and Kibosha, a cultural organization, having members all throughout the nation.

Cox, a graduate of the University of South Carolina, and Wood, who was graduated from the University of Nebraska, both of whom have been teaching at the Mid-Pacific Institute for the past three years and have also been taking graduate courses at the local university, will remain in the Orient following their tour of Japan. Cox will teach at Doshisha University at Kyoto, while Wood will join the faculty of Lingnan University of Canton, China.

Adachi, Osumi and Sasaki, all of whom are graduates of the University of Hawaii, are expected to return to Honolulu during the latter part of August. Adachi will represent the Japanese Students' Association of Hawaii on the tour, and he plans to attend the Imperial University at Tokyo for a few weeks to make a contact anese college undergraduates, in particular.

Extensive tests at the State College of Washington have shown that shock absorbers reduce the wear on automobile tires.

Norway possesses about 12,000,000 horsepower of potential hydroelectric power, of which about 1,500,000 have been developed.

Newspaper article (1930)

In the diary he kept during his trip, he was already considering what life was about and how to better this world. I admire my father because, at such a young age, he was already thinking and writing things of this nature. Some excerpts from that diary:

> *I was greatly impressed with the rapid reconstruction of Yokohama and Tokio. You remember that seven years ago those two cities were destroyed completely by the great earthquakes. Thousands of people including men, women, and children were killed. I had thought that I would see some traces of the catastrophe but I did not see any. It looked as though nothing had happened. Young people, there is a lesson in it. In life we meet all sorts of difficulties and hardships. Often times they seem to crush us to pieces, but are we going to let it overcome us? Let us awaken and fight the battles of life.*
>
> *I am of the opinion that the time has come when we ought to be working together hand in hand in making a better today and a glorious tomorrow discarding racial as well as religious animosities which are so prevalent in the world today.*
>
> *There is one word in Hawaii which we frequently use and of which we are very proud. It is no other than the word 'Aloha.' It is the spirit and soul of Hawaii. It is the spirit of goodwill, friendship, and all the things that are valuable in human relationships.*
>
> *We have been impressed by many good things in Japan. One primary purpose of coming to Japan is not only to see but to inculcate in ourselves the best that Japan has to offer. We Japanese youths of Hawaii keenly feel our responsibility, the responsibility of promoting and furthering friendship and*

understanding between the two great countries bordering the Pacific, Japan and America. I believe we can fulfill this responsibility only after having acquainted ourselves with the best in America and the best in Japan. ❦

CHAPTER 2

From Marriage through Early Ministries in Hilo and on Kaua'i

In 1930, upon his return from Japan, my father lived for four years in Waipahu Community House and worked under the Hawaiian Board of Missions (Waipahu, 'Ewa and Pearl City). He also worked part time, supervising the YMCA boys' club in the Leeward area, under the direction of Taichi Matsuno.

It was during this time that he met my mother, Janet Sadako Monden. Born in Nu'umalu, Kaua'i on January 25, 1912, she was the eldest of four daughters born to Masaji and Tsuyuko Monden. Later her family moved to Honolulu and lived at Kauluwela Lane, between School and Vineyard Streets, next to Nu'uanu Stream and across from the Honolulu Botanical Gardens. She and her younger sisters, Harriet, Margaret and Eloise, attended and graduated from McKinley High School. Upon graduation, she took business courses at the Margaret Dietz Commercial School.

I am not sure when, at what social gathering, or how my father met my mother. I wished I had asked them about this. People who knew my mother and her sisters told me they were attractive women. I especially wish I'd asked Father about this, especially now, having read in his yearbook that he had "a great weakness, and that is girls—he'd rather die than talk with one of the fair sex."

Father married my mother, a third-generation Japanese, on June 16, 1933, at Nu'uanu Japanese Church in Honolulu

Paul and Janet Osumi (1933)

(today the Nuʻuanu Congregational Church). After their marriage, my mother taught kindergarten in Waipahu. In August 1934, as my parents were getting ready to leave for the mainland for my father to attend graduate school, the Pearl City HI–Y members gave them an autograph book filled with short goodbye notes thanking my father and mother. Reading the autograph book, I see that the young people admired them greatly.

Graduate School

It was the fall of 1934 when my parents moved to Los Angeles so that Father could attend the University of Southern California (USC) School of Theology. Mother finished her kindergarten training at USC.

Getting married and then going to the mainland was a major decision in their lives. I do not know who encouraged my father to pursue his master's degree at USC, or how he decided to further his education. It is unclear to me if my mother was the influencer.

From 1934 to 1936, while attending USC, Father was a youth worker at the Los Angeles Union Church.

He graduated with honors and received his master of theology degree in June 1936. His master's thesis was entitled "A Comparative Study of the Missionary Impulse of Buddhism and Christianity." At the beginning of his thesis, he wrote, "Similarities between Buddhism and Christianity are more striking than differences. There is truth in every religion."

An excerpt from his thesis introduction:

> *As a young Japanese engaged in Christian work among his people who are mostly Buddhists, the writer is interested in Buddhism. To be an effective worker he must not be ignorant of the religion which most of his people profess. He must have an adequate understanding and knowledge of Buddhism. His attitude toward it must be one of sympathy and not of antagonism. He must know the relative values and merits of the two religions. So the writer had*

been wishing for some time to make a comparative study of Buddhism and Christianity. It is a comprehensive subject and will require years of study to fully comprehend the two religions. This thesis deals with one aspect of Buddhism and Christianity. The emphasis is placed mainly on the missionary impulse but other materials which are thought to be pertinent to the study are brought in. It has been found necessary to condense many parts of the study and leave out many details.

In such a study it is always difficult to be absolutely impartial and unprejudiced. Many Christians have written books on Buddhism but almost invariably they seem to have started with the assumption that Christianity is better than Buddhism. In this study a special care was taken to be impartial and to present an estimate that is fair and friendly.

Since the subject of the thesis covers large ground, the writer was faced with the problem of choosing a bibliography which was adequate and authoritative. He has read and studied extensively on the subject. He has drawn his materials freely from his personal experiences and observations in Japan and in America. He has visited churches and temples and has interviewed some people of authority. The condensing of an abundance of material was the greatest problem faced.

In its conclusion, he wrote:

It has been shown that both Christianity and Buddhism are missionary religions. To start with, their founders were missionaries. Jesus and Gautama realized their mission at about the same age.... One peculiar thing about them was that they made no distinction between classes of people. They sought to win all mankind. Their followers in turn

> *became missionaries. They crossed national boundaries and brought their messages of salvation to other nations.*
>
> *There is truth in every religion. Religion results from certain human hunger. Every form of religion seeks to satisfy certain basic human needs. There is truth in every faith and that truth springs from the same source. It springs from the Fountain of Truth…God. Forms of expression may vary but the root is the same. Forms of expression are accidents and they do vary but the truth is constant. The Spirit of God is at work everywhere.*

I include these excerpts from his thesis to demonstrate that my father had a very high respect for the Buddhist religion. He attended many Buddhist funerals and even spoke at some of the services. As a youth, I once asked him: "What should I do as a Christian? Can I attend Buddhist funerals and do the rituals conducted at the services?" His answer was yes, and he encouraged me to attend Buddhist funeral services. This was to pay respect to the deceased and family, he explained. Going through the rituals of the respective religions does not mean that I am not being a Christian. This, he stated, applies to all other religious services. I was happy and relieved to hear this, as most of my wife's family and relatives are Buddhist.

I recall that once a family member came to him and asked if he would provide a funeral service for one of their family members. They told him the deceased was not in good standing with his church, and the church refused to have a funeral service for him. Father told the family that he would gladly do the service, and the family was very grateful to my father. The deceased did not belong to the same faith as my father's church.

In his inspirational sayings, my father wrote that we belong to one race and that was the human race. He saw it as his mission to serve all people of all races, religions, statuses and ages.

Father never talked to me about the things I discovered

through my research. The more I researched my father's background, the more impressed I was with what he accomplished since he left Japan at the age of 14. I wondered: If I had been in his shoes, and at his age, could I have achieved what he did? My answer is no, and that is one of the reasons I wrote this book.

Hilo Japanese Christian Church

After my father graduated from USC, my parents returned to Hawai'i. It was June 18, 1936, and they were very happy to return to the Islands, where they lived in a cottage at the Hilo Boarding School. He was assigned to the Hilo Japanese Christian Church (now Church of the Holy Cross) on Kino'ole Street, where he became the youth minister under Rev. Chikatada Sagawa. He also helped with the Ola'a Christian Church and the Pāpa'ikou Christian Church, and developed youth programs under the direction of Rev. T. Markham Talmage of the First Foreign Church.

His work was related to general Christian programs under the Hawaiian Board of Missions. He loved to work with young people, and these tasks he was assigned must have given him great satisfaction. He was ordained in Hilo and licensed to perform marriage ceremonies in the Territory of Hawai'i on October 16, 1936.

The first documented sermon I found in his files was one he delivered on July 22, 1936, titled "Living Creatively." It spoke about how to live our lives; he saw this as one of the most important things we should all understand. Excerpts from this sermon are included in a later chapter.

In Hilo, where he was gaining recognition as an excellent speaker, he presided at a special service commemorating the 50th anniversary of mission work among the Japanese in the Territory of Hawai'i. He was also asked to be a keynote speaker at the opening session of the Christian Endeavor convention at Wailuku Japanese Church on Maui on March 11, 1938. His theme was "On the March," and he was lauded in the newspaper as having been an "excellent and challenging speaker, and all of his messages were well received."

Hilo Japanese Christian Church (1936)

He was active in the community and served as one of 32 local citizens on the Board of Directors of the Hilo Community Center.

My older brother, Paul S. Osumi, Jr., was born when my parents lived in Hilo. He later became an architect in Honolulu.

Līhu'e Christian Church

In July of 1938, my parents moved to Līhu'e, Kaua'i and my father became the minister at Līhu'e Japanese Christian Church (shortly after he became its minister, he changed the name to Līhu'e Christian Church). The church was affiliated with the Hawaiian Board of Missions. He succeeded the Rev. Chiyokichi Furuta, who became the minister of the Makiki Japanese Church in Honolulu. He worked closely with Rev. F. B. Withington, senior minister of Līhu'e Union Church and field secretary of the Hawaiian Board.

It is unclear where my parents lived in Līhu'e; their

address was P.O. Box 1268, Līhuʻe, Kauaʻi, Territory of Hawaiʻi. Father's bilingual abilities came into play on Kauaʻi, as he preached in English and then sometimes summarized the sermon in Japanese for the older generation of congregants.

In my research, I could not find any reference as to why he left Hilo for Līhuʻe. The only reason I can surmise is that when Rev. Chiyokichi Furuta became the minister at Makiki Japanese Church, the Hawaiian Board of Missions and the members of the church wanted and selected my father to fill his position.

In 1939, at the age of 34, Father was selected as one of seven delegates to represent Hawaiʻi at the World Christian Youth Conference in Amsterdam. Other delegates representing Hawaiʻi were: Hung Wai Ching, secretary of the University of Hawaiʻi YMCA; Abraham Akaka, student at Illinois Wesleyan College; Bertha Van Dyke, YWCA representative; Mineo Katagiri; Matthew Nahm, and someone from Central Union Church.

He left on June 23, 1939, on the vessel *Matsonia*, for three months. My father no doubt felt honored to represent Hawaiʻi at this international event where 1,500 youths from 71 countries were represented, although not Germany or Russia. On this trip, he visited Germany, France, England and Belgium.

He left Europe on August 15, before war was declared. Upon his return to Līhuʻe, he was quoted in the newspaper: "There was war talk everywhere and everywhere war preparations were much in evidence—blackouts and troop movements —but it seemed to me that in France and England was the crisis most keenly felt."

Father stated that while traveling through Germany, he met some young soldiers on a train. They seemed rather calm in expressing their opinion that war was bound to come, but as to when, they had no idea.

I found a few coins that he brought back from this trip. My parents must have had sentimental reasons for having kept them all these years.

Lihue Christian Church (1938)

Back in Līhu'e, with war clouds amassing ominously, he was issued an Alien Registration Receipt Card by the U.S. Department of Justice, Immigration and Naturalization Service, Alien Registration Division, Washington, D.C. His Registration Number was 2285998. Noted on the card:

> *To Registrant: Your registration under the Alien Registration Act, 1940, has been received and given the number shown above your name. This card is your receipt, and is evidence only of such registration. In writing to the Department of Justice about yourself, always give the number on this card.*

A Selective Service Registration Certificate shows he was duly registered on October 26, 1940. The government must have been concerned about all the Japanese immigrants living in the United States in 1940 to issue these Alien Registration Receipt Cards.

From 1938 to 1941, Father belonged to the Ministerial Association of Hawaiʻi, and from 1939 to 1941, to the Lions Club on Kauaʻi. On October 18, 1941, my parents' second child was born. That was me, Norman H. Osumi, born at Wilcox Hospital in Līhuʻe, Kauaʻi.

I was given the name Norman because when I was born, my father was in a meeting conducted by a Rev. Norman Schenck, secretary of the Board of the Hawaiian Evangelical Association. Someone suggested to my father that I be named after Rev. Schenck, and the reverend became my godfather after I was named after him. My middle name, Hideyuki, was given to me by my maternal grandfather.

To learn about Father's life in Līhuʻe, I visited Līhuʻe Christian Church on July 24, 2011 and met with older church members who remembered my father. They were Yoshie Shirai, Turk Tokita, Haruko Hiranako, Ruth Akama Wakayama, Fusae Masaki and others. They told me that my father was highly respected by church members and the community, and remembered that he was bilingual and spoke both Japanese and English very well. I learned that he gave sermons over the radio for people who may have missed his sermon on Sunday. They mentioned that he had been a substitute teacher for the Japanese Language School, which I was not aware of. They also said he was a handsome man, and that my mother was very attractive.

The Rev. Dr. James Fung, minister of Līhuʻe Christian Church, remembered Father's Today's Thoughts. His father would clip the daily sayings from the newspaper, paste them onto a sheet of paper and send them to his son while he was studying to become a minister. He said the daily sayings influenced his early ministry education.

I believe it was around this time that my father started to compile inspirational thoughts from Bible verses, and from his daily workings with people. He translated the verses into simple daily thoughts. Throughout his life, he had the gift of being able to translate his religious ideology into simple sayings and examples that everyone could relate to and understand. ✖

CHAPTER 3

Arrest After Pearl Harbor

It changed my father's and our family's lives forever when the United States declared war on Japan following the December 7, 1941 attack on Pearl Harbor. Father talked very little about what happened to him after the war started. I can only imagine what he went through as a 36-year-old Christian minister with a young family.

I have been able to reconstruct some of what happened to my father during the war years by gathering information from military archives, books, interviews with people who knew our family and especially Father at that time, and through letters and memos that my father both wrote and received.

The Secretary of War issued a warrant of arrest for Father on the same day Pearl Harbor was attacked. It read:

> *YOU ARE HEREBY COMMANDED to take the body of PAUL SUTEKICHI OSUMI alias SUTEKICHI OKADA on suspicion of being an alien enemy of the United States, and to detain said person pending final action by the Commanding General, Hawaiian Department, United States Army. This Warrant of Arrest is issued under the authority of the Secretary of War of the United States by his delegated agent this 7 day of December, 1941.*

Many thoughts go through my mind when I read this. First, Father was never known by the alias "Sutekichi Okada" in any of the documents I have in my possession. Sometimes I wonder if the government arrested the wrong person. Second, he was arrested "on suspicion of being an alien enemy," but it was never *proven* that he was an enemy alien in any of the government records I obtained. To the contrary, I have my father's Selective Service Card, which was issued on December 9, 1940 and classified him as 4-C (aliens not subject to military service); and another, dated October 15, 1943, which classified him as 4-F-H.

I believe that he was arrested because the United States Government identified all influential Japanese men before December 7, 1941, and thought these men would be a problem in Hawai'i if Japan invaded the Hawaiian Islands. The government thought that these men might align with the Japanese government and create a revolt in Hawai'i.

Father's letters indicate that he felt he was arrested because he was corresponding from Kaua'i with the Japanese Consulate of Honolulu. He thought the U.S. Government knew about this and used it against him, perhaps thinking he was providing coded messages to the Japanese government. In actuality, the reasons for his correspondence were innocuous. Prior to World War II, there was an active movement gaining strength in Hawai'i to encourage dual-citizen *nisei* (second-generation Japanese Americans) to expatriate from Japan. Before the war, the expatriation process on Kaua'i was being handled by Shujiro Takimoto, Līhu'e's Japanese Language School principal. To show his patriotism, Principal Takimoto climbed onto the school's rooftop each day to raise the American flag on the flagpole. Tragically, on October 22, 1940, he fell from the rooftop and died instantly.

There was a search for a replacement for Principal Takimoto, someone who could process the expatriation papers. My father was available at the time and literate enough in both Japanese and English to handle this responsibility, which was a complicated and cumbersome process. He was pressed into service to prepare the papers and correspondence with the Japanese Consulate of Honolulu.

I talked about this matter with people at the JCCH Resource Center, and others who were affected by Japanese internment during the war, and they believed that Father was on a government list before the war started because he was:

- A Japanese citizen (Asian-born persons could not become U.S. citizens until 1952, when Congress passed the Walter-McCarran Immigration and Nationality Act)

- Well-educated with a master's degree from the University of Southern California

- Influential in the Japanese community, and

- Highly respected on Kauaʻi.

He also spoke and wrote both Japanese and English very well and had corresponded with the Japanese Consulate before the war started.

I was determined to find out why the FBI considered him a dangerous person and included him on a list of Japanese people they wanted to apprehend even before the war started.

I began my search on September 18, 2007, when I first wrote to the late U.S. Senator Daniel Inouye's office for assistance in receiving copies of Father's FBI files under the "Freedom of Information Act." I also corresponded with a Mr. David M. Hardy of the Records Management Division of the FBI in Washington D.C. Mr. Hardy replied that, after a search of the automated and manual indices, no records on my father could be found.

On March 13, 2009, an article in the *Honolulu Advertiser* stated that the FBI's file-searching methods were "woeful" and that no records turned up for 66 percent of Freedom of Information requests. The same day the article appeared, I wrote again to Senator Inouye's office asking for help and attached the FBI correspondence as well as the *Advertiser* article.

A legislative assistant from Senator Inouye's office, who had been in contact with Mr. John Fox, an FBI investigative historian, responded. He told me there were only a few documents referencing Rev. Paul Osumi, and that they had been destroyed many years ago. The legislative assistant also gave me Mr. Fox's telephone number, in case I wanted to speak with him. I did not call Mr. Fox since I didn't think he was going to give me further information about my father.

Father was branded a "consular agent"—a representative of the Japanese government—and was rounded up with other Japanese declared "enemy aliens," a label that was never proven. He was taken to the Kauaʻi jail near Kapaʻa on December 7, 1941, by two FBI agents.

I cannot imagine what my father went through when he was picked up at his home and immediately taken away without explanation. My mother must have been totally afraid. My parents never spoke to me about that day or about what went through their minds.

Alien Registration Receipt Card (1942), County Jail, Wailua, Kauai, T.H. Address

The case against my father was presented by FBI Special Agent W. C. Ingman, who stated that my father replaced Rev. Furuta, the former minister of Līhuʻe Christian Church who had been identified as a "consular agent." Agent Ingman said Father had received his first certificate of appointment from the Japanese Consulate about three years earlier, and had received his last one in January 1941 for a period of two years. According to Ingman, my father completed 10 military deferments as a consular agent, and resigned his position about one week after President Franklin D. Roosevelt's executive order on July 25, 1941, that froze all Japanese assets in the United States. It appeared the FBI could not provide documents to support Agent Ingman's allegations.

In his letters, Father wrote that he "was not a consular agent" and that this was a technical error. He never stated in his letters that he processed any military deferments. He did write that he helped people holding dual citizenship who wanted to renounce their Japanese citizenship; he wrote their requests to the Japanese Consulate.

On January 9, 1942, at 1:10 p.m., a proceeding of a Board of Officers and Civilians met in Līhuʻe to hear evidence and make recommendations regarding internment of enemy aliens, dual citizens and citizens. Members present were: Mr. C. E. S. Burns, Mr. Hector Moir, Mr. Lindsey Faye and Major George W. Tivy, executive and recorder.

Mr. W. C. Ingman, the FBI special agent, presented the Government's case against 41 Japanese men, with my father listed as number 30. He stated that all of the men were consular agents of the Japanese government. After describing their duties, he said that each of the men had been issued a certificate of appointment bearing the seal of the Japanese Consul General. These certificates deemed that the men were entrusted to act as consular agents for two years. Mr. Ingman further stated: "These men are chosen from leading alien Japanese in the communities and are 'believed' to act as espionage agents or observers. This has been verified in one instance." He concluded that he did not have anything on the records other than the fact that they were consular agents. The proceeding ended at 2:15 p.m.

I believe that the FBI was afraid of any Japanese person with influence in the community. I could not find any records showing that my father was a consular agent. Also, charging 41 men as enemy agents because of a single "verified" instance of espionage, which was never proven, was highly suspect. The Consul General's certificate did not imply that the appointed were diplomatic officers of Japan, and I believe they did not need to register as agents of foreign principals. The Japanese Consulate appointed them to help Japanese citizens, living throughout the Islands, complete forms that needed to be filed. I believe the Japanese Consulate issued the certificate to Father although he did not request or sign any document indicating he wanted to be a consular agent. Throughout his entire internment, he could not understand why he had been arrested.

My father had an individual hearing before the Board of Officers and Civilians on January 26, 1942, at 9:11 a.m. Under oath, he testified that he "performed work by the Japanese consular agents. The main purpose of this work was to renounce citizens of Japan." He did not say he was a consular agent. He said he processed seven cases of renouncing citizenship, one death report and birth certificates. Although he returned the Japanese Consul General's certificate of appointment, which was not signed, to the consulate in July 1941, he said he continued to help people with their papers by typing for them and telling them how to file. He also declared "100 percent" loyalty to the United States, and said that he would help the United States against Japan, but not Japan against the United States.

At the end of his hearing, the Board found:

1. *That the internee is a citizen of the Empire of Japan.*

2. *That the internee is not loyal to the Empire of Japan.*

3. *That the internee is apparently not engaged in any subversive activities.*

   Recommends: that the internee be paroled to the custody of Reverend Frederic Withington, Līhu'e, Kaua'i.

The Board meeting adjourned at 9:45 a.m., just 34 minutes after it started.

Seven weeks later, though, on March 18, the Office of the Assistant Chief of Staff for Military Intelligence in Honolulu issued this recommendation: "We the undersigned representatives of our respective Intelligence Bureau, do not concur in the recommendations of the Board and recommend that Paul Sutekichi Osumi alias Sutekichi Okada, be interned." It was signed by Lt. Col. George W. Bicknell of Military Intelligence; I. H. Mayfield of the District Intelligence Office, 14th Naval District; and R. L. Shivers of the FBI. I did not find any military or FBI records explaining why they overturned the Board's decision; the FBI later destroyed all records.

On March 19, 1942, the following day, Lt. Gen. Emmons, Department Commander, Office of the Military Governor, ordered my father's internment. My father's residence on April 5 of that year was shown as the County Jail, Wailua, Kauaʻi. In a testament to Father's excellent standing in the community, many prominent people on Kauaʻi signed a letter, dated April 7, 1942, urging Lt. Gen. Emmons to reconsider.

After listing his personal and educational history in Hawaiʻi, the letter said:

> *Expatriation for Hawaiian-born Japanese was felt by Osumi to be of the highest importance and considered assistance to such young people part of his work as a minister. When a letter arrived from the Japanese Consulate in Honolulu authorizing him as a correspondent he thought of it only as a means of securing unquestioned American citizenship for the many young people who came to him for help. He never asked for such consular connection, neither did he acknowledge the letter, nor enter into any agreement with the Consulate. When he discussed some of the problems of his work with the members of his church and the Hawaiian Board, he was urged to continue to help in what was openly believed by all*

of us to be a patriotic undertaking. We feel confident that at no time did he think himself as an agent of the Japanese Government, but only as our helper in an important service for our young American citizens. We have probably no young Japanese Christian leader in Hawaii whose influence has been more constructive in Americanization then Osumi. People of all races respect his leadership, which during these unstable times would be a definite force in the maintenance of law and order. If we as a body of citizens may stand sponsor for him, we shall be glad to assume this responsibility. We earnestly ask your consideration of Osumi's case.

Signed by: C. E. S. Burns, Andrew Gross, Dwight O. Welch, W. P. Alexander, Elsie H. Wilcox, Chas. A. Rice, Wm. Henry Rice, L. A. Faye, H. Mcd. Moir, Charles Keahi, Mabel I. Wilcox, and A. H. Waterhouse.

On April 13, Norman C. Schenck, general secretary, the Board of Hawaiian Evangelical Association, wrote to Lt. Gen. Delos C. Emmons, military governor, Territory of Hawai'i:

Please find enclosed a letter signed by twelve citizens of the island of Kauai in behalf of Rev. Paul Osumi, who is being held in protective custody at present. The twelve names attached herewith include four plantation managers, a former sheriff, two former senators, a Hawaiian pastor, a welfare worker, a Y.M.C.A. executive and the commissioner of education for Kauai. We are sure of their loyal Americanism. They are sure of the value to any community of Rev. Paul Osumi. As General Secretary of the Hawaiian Evangelical Association, I am honored to forward to you this letter with these signatures, and as an American myself of three hun-

dred and fifty years ancestry from Holland, I should like to add my request that Mr. Osumi be released. I sincerely believe that he is loyal to America and true to his profession as a Christian minister.

Miss Elsie Wilcox, Mr. W. P. Alexander and Rev. Frederic B. Withington, pastor of Līhu'e Union Church, all wrote individual letters testifying to my father's good standing and urging the reversal of the decision to intern him.

Despite their best efforts, though, my father remained interned, and it was around April 10 of that year my mother, brother and I returned to Honolulu to live with my mother's parents at 1571 Kauluwela Lane. My mother told me that once the government apprehended my father, many people stayed away from her, afraid that if government agents saw them associating with her they would be arrested as well.

After Father was arrested, the military took over the church and used it for its purposes.

 A few people did step up to help during this most difficult time. Mrs. Yoshie Shirai, a Līhu'e Christian Church member, drove my mother around and took her to see Father when he was in jail, because my mother did not drive. Mr. Turk Tokita, another Līhu'e Christian Church member, told me that when he tried to see my father in jail, the guards refused to let him because he was Japanese and the guards were racially prejudiced.

I am very appreciative to Miss Elsie Wilcox, who helped my parents with financial support and encouragement during the war years. My father dedicated the *God in the Desert* one-minute sermons he published in 1947 to her. ✺

CHAPTER 4

Sand Island Detention Camp and Lordsburg Internment Camp, New Mexico

On June 6, 1942, my father was transferred from the Kaua'i County Jail to Sand Island Detention Camp in Honolulu. I cannot imagine how he felt—a Christian minister who did everything to help people in Hawai'i and to live by American values—being treated like a criminal. In a letter dated June 12, 1942, E. E. Walker, Captain, U.S. Army, Office of Military Governor, Territory of Hawaii, told him that "after careful consideration of your case by the hearing board and reviewing authorities, it appears necessary to intern you for the duration of the war, and your internment has been so ordered by the Department Commander under date of 19 March 1942."

He must have felt devastated after reading this letter. He lived and preached a Christian and American way of living and did nothing against the United States, and yet the government considered him an enemy agent. He had a family, and now there was enormous uncertainty in his life. I believe he relied on his Christian faith during this darkest period of his life.

The living conditions at Sand Island were not good. After reading the book *Life Behind Barbed Wire* by Yasutaro Soga, a first-generation Japanese in Hawai'i, I realized that the internees at Sand Island were not treated very well and that my father had to endure this.

The Government granted my mother permission to visit Father at Sand Island on June 21. She was told not to bring any gifts or food. At this time, my father's health, as recorded

```
                811TH MILITARY POLICE COMPANY
                       Sand Island, T. H.

                                              June 15  1942

  Mrs. Paul Osumi
  1571 Kauluwela Lane
  Honolulu

         You may have the opportunity to visit   Paul
    S. Osumi                Sunday,   21 June 1942

  1942.  Be at Pier #12, the Castle & Cooke Freight Office at 1:00
  o'clock, and transportation will be furnished to Sand Island.
           Please do not bring any gifts or food stuffs.


                                        S. H. Spillner
                                       Lt. S. H. SPILLNER
                                       1st Lieut., Infantry,
                                       Detention Camp,
                                       Sand Island, T.H.
```

Government visitation letter (1942)

by the military, was good. Unfortunately, after that my mother was denied from seeing him again before he was transferred to the mainland.

On June 22, 1942, Father left Honolulu on a transport with 38 other Japanese men who were interned at Sand Island. They joined hundreds of others as "Group Four," which totaled 702 internees, eight of them women. Group Four reached Angel Island in San Francisco on June 29. Because he was bilingual, my father served as interpreter for the FBI and the Army during his detainment in Hawai'i, while on the transport to the mainland (where one prisoner jumped overboard, creating an emergency), and during their stay at Angel Island.

On July 5, he was transported by train from Angel Island to the Lordsburg Internment Camp in Hidalgo County, New Mexico, an all-male camp where he arrived on July 27. Internment camps were like prison camps, while relocation camps were where West Coast Japanese families were relocated to live.

```
LORDSBURG INTERNMENT CAMP
   LORDSBURG, NEW MEXICO

PAUL SUTEKICHI OSUMI
Chief Secretary of Compound 3

Captain Caryle L. Whitemarsh
Commander of Compound 3
```

Lordsburg Internment Camp ID card, Lordsburg, New Mexico (1942)

In my father's files, I found a memo he wrote about the "Treatment of Internees from Hawaii," which covered the period from leaving Honolulu to his stay at Lordsburg, New Mexico. He wrote:

> *We left Honolulu on a transport on June 22 and reached San Francisco on June 29. During the trip we feel that we, thirty-nine internees, were ill-treated. We request improvements in the treatment of the internees when they are being transported from Honolulu to the mainland. In spite of the fact that we fully cooperated with the army authorities like gentlemen in observing all laws and regula-*

tions pertaining to us internees we were treated high-handedly as criminals by the guards who accompanied us. We cite the following to substantiate our claim of ill-treatment.

<u>*Coming To The Mainland:*</u>

1) *When we were being interned at the Sand Island Detention Camp in Honolulu harbor, we were told that we could meet our families. We were overjoyed and were waiting for the day with great expectation. But suddenly on the day before the visiting day, the order to send us away to the mainland came. We were sent to the boat on the following morning (Sunday, which was visiting day) but the boat did not sail until Monday evening. Visitation could have been permitted. The whole thing was cruel beyond words. If they had no intention of permitting us to see our families, why not tell us from the very beginning that we could not see our families?*

2) *In the boat we were placed in a dark, unsanitary quarters in G. Deck at the head of the boat.*

3) *The latrine facilities were totally lacking in our quarters. We had to use latrines two decks above. But we were not free to use them.*

4) *During the day we were permitted to go to the latrines thirteen at a time every three hours. But each time we were not given enough time. One of the guards went so far as to poke us with his stick, ordering us to hurry.*

5) *During the night we weren't permitted to go up to the latrines. We were given only a bucket for this purpose for the night.*

6) Due to the fact that we were not given the free use of the latrines the sick among us as well those who were seasick suffered terribly.

7) We were permitted to take a shower bath once every three days but the water used was the ocean water. Even for washing our faces in the morning fresh water was not given. We had to use ocean water for this purpose.

8) An aged man among us was in bed with cold. Though he explained in detail his condition, the guards forced him to get up and made him take shower against his will.

9) The language the guards used at us was extremely vulgar and their attitude toward us was lacking in human sympathy.

10) We believe that the officers in charge should have retrained the guards. We request that the officer in charge visit the internees once a day from now on.

<u>On The Train:</u>

The train for the transportation of us internees from San Francisco to Lordsburg was evidently for criminals. All windows and doors were screened with heavy wire-nets. The inside of the car was dirty and unsanitary and the car was almost like a freight car.

<u>Miscellaneous:</u>

1) For those who do not understand English, we request that we be permitted to obtain books, magazines, and newspapers, so long as they are not anti-American. The other internees from the

mainland are being permitted to obtain them freely. We want to be treated the same.

2) The mails to and from Hawaii are very slow. From the clipper, mails require over a month for one way. We urgently request that the mails to and from Hawaii be handled more speedily.

3) The internees from the mainland can freely and in short time obtain articles as well as cash from their relatives and friends but we from Hawaii are greatly inconvenienced in not being able to obtain them freely due to the distance. We request that we be permitted to obtain the necessary money and keep it here and buy articles through the mail orders.

4) We understand that many articles which were taken away from us such as identification cards, mimeographs, letters, safety razors and blades, are to be kept by the authorities. We request that they be returned to us.

5) The suitcase belonging to Mr. Matsujiro Ohtani of our group was lost. The suitcases were taken to the Immigration Station on the morning of Feb 18 according to word received from his family. The value of the content of the suitcase was approximately $250. The suitcase is still missing. We request that this be investigated.

6) Request regarding joint-detention of internees with their families be applied, as far as internees from Hawaii are concerned, only to those who so desire.

This is the first memo where my father stated his dissatisfaction with the treatment he and other internees received. Father must have been very upset to write this memo about situations such as when he could not see my mother before being shipped to the mainland and the way the military authorities handled visitation for the internees.

Upon the group's arrival by train in Lordsburg, New Mexico, at 1:15 a.m. on July 27, an incident occurred that greatly affected my father, and which he documented in great detail. Two men in the group were sick, and they were asked to come forward by the authorities. The rest of the men proceeded to march from the station to the camp, and when they reached the outside of the camp fence, many of them heard several rifle shots.

By that evening, it was rumored that the two sick men had been shot, but the army physician said the men were well taken care of. Early the next morning, though, the physician reported that one of the two sick men had, indeed, been shot to death. Later it was learned that both men were shot and killed.

Leaders of the internees' group convened to discuss what to do. Camp authorities declared that a funeral service for the two men would be held at four o'clock that same day. The leaders asked the authorities to have the men's bodies examined in the presence of physicians and leaders from the internee group, but that request was denied. The leaders decided they would seek a solution to the problem when the Spanish consul arrived. The Spanish consul often acted as a hearing board for internees' grievances during the war.

My father proceeded to gather information about the sick men and their conditions, as well as statements from internees who knew the men. He also documented the proceedings of a meeting about the shootings and their aftermath, which was held on November 18 with a Lt. Mitchell. At this meeting, they learned that the guard who shot the two men was found not guilty. Also, Lt. Mitchell said that the sick men tried to run away—but the internees knew that those two men were not capable of running. One had tuberculosis, and the other was suffering from spinal paralysis and had to stoop and take short steps when walking.

After reading about this incident, I wonder what my father thought of the American justice system and the honesty of American citizens and soldiers. He never spoke to me about this incident, and continued to believe in the American way even after the war. I believe he must have held on to his Christian belief of "forgiveness," even when he saw injustice being done.

On October 7, when he'd been at Lordsburg a few months, Father wrote to Edward J. Ennis, director of the Alien Enemy Control Unit at the Department of Justice in Washington D.C., to present his case, and he asked to be released. In the letter, he recounted his educational and professional history in Hawai'i and listed 19 people who could vouch for his outstanding character. He pledged his loyalty to the United States. He denied the charge on which he was arrested: That he was a consular agent for Japan. He stated emphatically that, "I was arrested and interned on the charge that I was a consular agent. But I NEVER WAS."

My father asked to be given special consideration, and, if he could not return to his family, to at least be permitted to live at Gila Relocation Center in Arizona, where there was a need for Christian ministers. He closed the letter with these words:

> *My heart is with America and all my words and conduct will be in accordance with the best interests of America. My main concern will be to spiritually minister to the people of the camp. My work is to be the servant of God in spreading Christ's gospel. And I want to go where I can be of best service to him.*

When the 1942 Christmas holidays arrived, though, Father was still at Lordsburg. He seems to have spent much of his time teaching English to the internees and serving as their interpreter.

He wrote, too, that the camp wanted to put on a Christmas program and needed a Mary. Since he was young, they asked him to be Mary. He shaved off his mustache and put on makeup. The men could not believe they were seeing such a pretty face, and had to come up to him after the program to have a closer look at who he really was.

My father is mentioned in the book *Life behind Barbed Wire*, by Yasutaro Soga:

> *Rev. Sutekichi Osumi from Hawaii devoted himself not only to the pastors' association but also to his work as the chief secretary of the third battalion, a barracks chief, and an English lecturer. Among the many classes held at the camp, one of the most important was English (Rev. Sutekichi Osumi). I had the greatest respect for him.*

CHAPTER 5

Released to Gila Relocation Camp

Finally, Father was released from Lordsburg Internment Camp in New Mexico to the Gila Relocation Center in Arizona. I can only imagine how relieved and very happy he must have been.

Lordsburg was like a prisoner-of-war camp, holding men who were considered enemies of the United States. The Gila Relocation Center, on the other hand, held Japanese families who were removed from their homes along the West Coast due to Executive Order 9044.

There continued to be many attempts at getting him released, first from Lordsburg and then from his life at Gila, lasting until the war ended.

Rev. Royden Susu-Mago, a very close friend and a minister at the Gila Relocation Center, was instrumental in having my father released from Lordsburg and relocated to Gila in order to serve as youth minister. Rev. Susu-Mago

Gila Relocation Camp, Gila Rivers, Arizona (1943)

wrote to the United States government for his release. His letter to Honorable Edward J. Ennis, Deptartment of Justice, Washington, D.C., was dated September 29, 1942:

Dear Sir:

>*I am writing about the Rev. Mr. Paul Osumi of Lihue, Kauai, T.H. He is a fine Christian minister for whose character and integrity I can vouch. I have known him over ten years as an outstanding man. At the present time, he is interned at the Enemy Alien Internment Camp at Lordsburg, New Mexico, for reasons unknown to him. I am sure that a man of his integrity could not be disloyal to this nation.*
>
>*Will you kindly review his case once more and if it can be done, will you release him to the custody of the Christian ministers of this Relocation Center? At the present time, I am the only Nisei (citizen) pastor here. We are in great need of a pastor for Camp #1 to head the young people's religious work there. I am sure you will agree with me that Mr. Osumi can do an inestimable good for the children and young people of this center. Furthermore, the ministers—there are seven of us—will hold ourselves personally responsible for the Rev. Mr. Osumi's utterances. If he should ever violate our trust we shall surely return him to the FBI without hesitation.*
>
>*I shall appreciate greatly your prompt attention to this request.*
>
>*Most respectfully yours,*
>*(Rev.) Royden Susu-Mago*

Rev. Susu-Mago then submitted a request to Lt. Gen. Delos C. Emmons, Fort Shafter, Honolulu, Territory of Hawaiʻi. His letter was dated November 19, 1942:

Dear Sir:

I am writing in the matter of the Reverend Mr. Paul Osumi, pastor of Lihue Japanese Christian Church, now interned at Lordsburg, New Mexico. I have known Mr. Osumi for over ten years and in all that time I have never heard him utter anything detrimental to the interests of the United States. Although I do not know what the specific charges against him are, I am sure he has no evil intentions toward undermining the morale of United States citizens.

If there is any possibility I, speaking in behalf of the Christian Ministerial Council of Rivers Community, Arizona, should like to plead for a rehearing of Mr. Osumi's case. The reason for this is that here at Rivers we have great need for an English-speaking Christian minister to reside in Camp #1 which is without supply. If Mr. Osumi's release from Lordsburg can be obtained, we want him to work among the young people in Camp #1 of this Relocation Center. The Ministerial Council will take full responsibility for Mr. Osumi and if he should say or do anything subversive we will feel it our duty to report him immediately to the Army or FBI. We are asking for Mr. Osumi, however, because we are convinced that he will prove himself worthy of our trust and confidence in him.

We are aware of the grave responsibility resting upon your shoulders as a defender of that most important outpost of American Democracy, and beseech God's grace upon you. We pray for the speedy return of peace which shall be truly just and

> *durable, so that the sacrifice of blood will not have been made in vain.*
>
> *Hope that you will find it possible to give favorable consideration to the request of this letter, I am*
>
> > *Most sincerely yours.*
> > *Royden Susu-Mago, Pastor*

I did not find any documentation indicating how Rev. Susu-Mago knew my father was at Lordsburg.

Father wrote a subsequent letter requesting his release to Maj. E. E. Walker, Enemy Alien Processing Center, Immigration Station, Honolulu, Territory of Hawai'i, dated January 14, 1943:

> *Sometime ago we received a circular from Mr. Edward J. Ennis, director of Alien Enemy Control Unit, Department of Justice, in which he states that it is possible under a recent regulation for either the internee, a member of his family, or an interested person to make application for a rehearing.*
>
> *I wrote a letter presenting my case to the Justice Department, sometime ago. The letter was referred to the War Department and I got the instruction to write directly to you as my case was handled by the Military Governor in Hawaii.*
>
> *So, I am writing you this letter of petition asking you to have my case reviewed. I feel that I am a real victim of circumstances and that I don't belong here. Please permit me to briefly present my case.*
>
> *(He covered who he was, his education, his work as a Christian minister, listed nineteen people who would testify as to his character, and his loyalty to the United States.)*

> *I was arrested and interned on the charge I was a consular agent. But I NEVER WAS. Believing that the church young people should renounce their Japanese citizenship, I helped many of them expatriate. I only helped them write papers to the Japanese consulate and to the Board of Health. As a Christian minister, I thought it was my duty to help them. Rev. Withington knew that I was doing this. The former pastor of the Church was doing this for more than ten years. I stepped into his shoes when I accepted the pastorate. It was one of the things required of the minister and besides I felt that it was a good thing to America to have these dual citizens to give up their Japanese citizenship. Great was my surprise when I was branded as a consular agent.*
>
> *Of course, nothing will make me happier than to be released and sent back to my family in Hawaii. But if this is not possible I would like to be permitted to live in the Gila Relocation Center in Arizona. I have my friend, Rev. Royden Susu-Mago from Hawaii there and he told me that Christian ministers are badly needed there especially in this Camp One. What I want more than anything else is to be cleared of my charge.*

Rev. Royden Susu-Mago sent my father a postcard dated January 8, 1943, which I believe he received after he wrote the previous letter:

> *Dear Paul:*
>
> > *Just heard from the Military Governor's office in Honolulu saying they have recommended you for parole to live and work as a minister in this center. If the Provost Marshal General in Washington approves, you will be with us soon. I have written to the Provost Marshal General. This*

> *Military Governor's Executive Officer, Lt. Col. Wm. R. C. Morrison, says that you will have to apply for parole to the Provost Marshal General, Washington, D.C., too, and ask that you be allowed to live and do Christian work in this center. Do that right away, today, and let me know about developments. Good luck and God bless you. Happy New Year! Ask for parole, not a rehearing. Royden*

Father wrote to the Provost Marshal General, Washington, D.C., on January 28:

> "*I have just received a notice saying that the Commanding General, Hawaiian Department, has recommended my parole to live and work as a Christian minister at the Relocation Center at Rivers, Arizona. I was also directed to apply to Your Honor for parole.*"

The Provost Marshal General then directed Brig. Gen. B. M. Bryan, director of the Alien Division, to reply to my father. In his letter dated February 2, 1943, he wrote:

> *Accomplishment of your parole is dependent upon the willingness of the Immigration and Naturalization Service to accept its general supervision and upon the willingness of the War Relocation Authority to admit you to the Center at Rivers, Arizona.*

Father then wrote to Mr. Willard F. Kelly, Immigration and Naturalization Service, Department of Justice, Philadelphia, Pennsylvania, on February 10, 1943:

> *I have just received word from Brigadier General B. M. Bryan, director of the Alien Division in the office of the Provost Marshal General, informing me that I was recommended to be paroled by the Provost Marshal General and the Commanding General of*

> *the Hawaiian Department and that my case was referred to Your Honor.*
>
> *I hereby respectfully beg Your Honor to accept the supervision of my parole.*

A letter from my father to the War Relocation Authority in Rivers, Arizona was dated February 15, 1943:

> *I have received a letter from Brigadier General B. M. Bryan, director of the Alien Division in the Office of the Provost Marshal General, informing me that I was recommended to be paroled by the Provost Marshal General, the Justice Department, and the Commanding General of the Hawaiian Department and that my parole was forwarded to the Immigration and Naturalization Service, Philadelphia, Pennsylvania, that it accept general supervision of my parole at the War Relocation Center at Rivers, Arizona.*
>
> *Rev. Royden Susu-Mago with the backing of the Christian ministers at your center helped me secure my parole so that I could come to the Center to assist in the Christian work.*
>
> *I hereby respectfully beg you to admit me to your Center. I am sure Rev. Royden Susu-Mago will testify as to my loyalty, Character, and activities.*

My father was finally given approval to be paroled on March 3, 1943, and left Lordsburg for Gila on March 25. He arrived at Gila the morning of March 26 and stayed with Rev. Susu-Mago until March 31. His address was Camp 1, 16-9-B. Father then moved to Camp 1, 16-8-A on March 31, where he moved in with Mr. Clifford Nakadegawa, who was preparing for ministry. He became my father's assistant in doing Christian work at Gila.

As the youth minister at the Canal Christian Church in the Gila Relocation Center, Father was very busy. His calendar of events for each month at Gila was as follows:

1) Hospital Visitation
2) Sunday School
3) Preaching Services
4) Counseling
5) Young People's Work
    a. Pilgrim Fellowship
    b. Young People's Fellowship
6) Prayer Meetings

The Board of Home Missions of the Congregational and Christian Churches in New York provided him a monthly allowance of $22, starting in April 1943.

Canal Christian Church, Gila Relocation Camp (1943)

Even after he left Lordsburg Internment Camp, my father maintained a close relationship with his former camp. He sent artificial lilies, made by the women in Gila, to Lordsburg for its Easter service. The camp's chaplain, Edward O. DeCamp, was very appreciative and sent a thank you letter for the lilies.

I was surprised to obtain Father's medical records from the military archives and learn that on February 5, 1944, he contracted valley fever (a fever caused by a fungal growth in his lungs), which caused him to have pleurisy. He ended up in a barracks hospital, where he was very ill. His attending physician was Dr. K. Kiyasu.

I can only imagine that he did not understand why he was imprisoned and separated from his family, thousands of miles away, and lying ill, sad and lonely in a barrack hospital. He held on to his Christian belief that God was there with him.

On March 22, 1944, the War Relocation Authority, Gila River Project, Rivers, Arizona, requested my father sign a document that asked, *"Will you swear to abide by the laws of the U.S. and to take no action which would in any way interfere with the war efforts of the United States?"* He signed it with a yes. I wonder why the Government asked him to sign this document, when he had already written letters to the Government stating his loyalty to the United States.

When my mother learned of Father's illness, she decided to take my brother and me to the Gila Relocation Center. Ms. Elsie Wilcox, senator of the Territory of Hawai'i, was instrumental in obtaining government approval for us to go to my father in Gila. My parents were so blessed to have Ms. Wilcox's support, which she provided from the time the war started through to the end of the war. Without her help, I am not sure what our family's fate would have been.

We left Honolulu for San Francisco on July 22, 1944. We were on a cargo ship that also had passenger accommodations. My mother was very seasick and was in bed for most of the trip. My brother, Paul, therefore, took care of me. My mother told me she was not sure how my brother managed, since he was only seven years old and I was only three.

Osumi family in front of barrack unit, Gila Relocation Camp (1945)

We took the Southern Pacific Railroad from San Francisco to Casa Grande and joined our father in Gila on August 4, 1944. I have vague memories of riding on the train and hope I can someday take the same train route again.

We became close family friends with the Yuki family, who lived in the same block in Gila. That family, who had three daughters, took care of my brother and me while my mother attended to my father in the camp's medical facility. Father was discharged from the hospital on October 30.

Seven months later, in May of 1945, my mother and brother were in bed for two weeks with valley fever. Since I have no further information about their illness, I assume they both recovered quickly.

While he was in Gila, my father wrote condensed sermons for young boys and girls joining the United States Army to take with them as they left the relocation camp for war in Europe. After the war, and with Father's permission, Ms. Ruth Isabel Seabury compiled 40 of these one-minute sermons for devotional reading and bound them into a booklet called *God in the Desert*. This booklet, printed in 1947, was intended for a wider audience. (See Chapter 6.)

A collection called *Rich Life in Barren Desert*, containing 60 sermons, local illustrations and references, was discussed in July 1945 by the Commission on Evangelism and Devotional Life, New York, who planned to print it as a booklet. My father's memoirs were also referred to in this booklet, but I could not locate a copy. I did find the foreword he wrote for this booklet, and 22 of the sermons, in his files.

The foreword, dated July, 1945, from Gila Relocation Center, Rivers, Arizona:

> *Our church young people are now scattered far and wide. Many have gone out to resettle in communities all over the United States. With the lifting of the ban, some have ventured back to California in spite of the night-riding terrorist. Most boys have joined the Armed Forces and are now serving Uncle Sam*

> *in far-flung theaters of war in Pacific and Europe. A few girls have joined the WACS.*
>
> *They all write back and say that they can never forget the wonderful Christian fellowship they had in the old Canal Church. The life they had lived here will be their cherished memory.*
>
> *While they were here their faith was on trial—their faith in democracy and God. Without charge and without trial they had been held for nearly two years and had been denied the freedom of other Americans. Thinking that they were forsaken by their country and by their God, they were in despair.*
>
> *But God tempered them "in life's hot flames and beat them to an edge with many grievous stroke." Their faith in democracy has been restored. Their loyalty has been proved in blood in battlefields. They have come out with a firmer and sounder faith in God.*
>
> *These are "the distilled Essence" of the sermons preached to these young people in a bare barrack chapel where the benches were made of scrap wood and the altar was improvised.*
>
> *The date of closing of the camp is fast drawing near. May this booklet serve as a reminder of the rich life lived in this barren desert.*

I found five 3-1/2 x 5-1/2 cards in Father's files, each printed with "A One Minute Sermon." I don't know how many of these sermons were printed while he was in Gila.

On January 5, 1945, J. Leslie Dunstan, general secretary, the Board of the Hawaiian Evangelical Association in Honolulu, submitted a request to Lt. R. J. Hoogs, Travel Section, Office of Internal Security, Honolulu. The request was that Father and Rev. Masayoshi Wakai, another Christian minister, return to Hawaiʻi. On February 1, 1945, he submitted an Application for

A One Minute Sermon
REV. PAUL OSUMI

Do You Take Yourself Seriously?

With a twinkle in his eye, Socrates used to tell his friends that his wife had taught him patience. If he came home late, his fiery wife would pour a bucket of cold water over his head. But Socrates took it philosophically and did not take himself or his wife seriously.

The strain of life which we are called upon to bear these days becomes heavy and we tend to lose our sense of proportion. Life becomes a solemn affair and we become irritable and inpatient with others.

Dr. Stanley Jones says, "When I get tense and take myself too seriously, I deliberately walk to the looking glass and burst out laughing. Even if I do not feel like laughing, I feel more like it when I see the man in the glass laughing."

Some one prayed, "O Lord, grant us a true sense of humor. May its kindly light and its healing power relax life's tension."

Life will be happier if we all ask God every day to give us this grace of laughter. "A merry heart maketh a cheerful countenance." (Proverbs 15:13).

A sentence sermon: *"Take everything in life seriously, if you like, but never yourself."*

—Joseph F. Newton.

A One Minute Sermon

Priority to Enter Hawaii from Mainland in the name of my father and Rev. Wakai.

On May 25, 1945, Father wrote to Brig. Gen. Wm. R. C. Morrison, Executive, Office of Internal Security, Iolani Palace Grounds, Honolulu, Territory of Hawai'i:

> *Dear Sir:*
>
> *We made our application for the permission to return to Hawaii in January through Dr. J. Leslie Dunstan, General Secretary of the Hawaiian Board of Missions. We have not yet heard whether we will be permitted to return to Hawaii or not. We are anxious to know in view of the fact that the relocation center in which we are now residing is to close in the near future and we will have to make our plans accordingly.*
>
> *I was detained immediately after the outbreak of the war in Lihue where I had been serving as pastor of the Lihue Christian Church. I understand that I was recommended for parole by the review board in Kauai and that a special petition for parole was drawn by a group of influential people in Kauai and sent to the Military Governor of Hawaii. But due to some circumstances I was brought over to the mainland to be interned. In March of 1943 I was paroled and since then I have been living in the Gila Relocation Center. I was one of the first Hawaiian internees to be paroled. My wife, Janet, and two children, Paul aged 7, and Norman aged 3, came to join me here in August of 1944. In the meantime I have received calls from two churches in Hawaii to be their pastor, the Paia Congregational Church and the Waialua Pilgrim Church, through the Hawaiian Board of Missions. I was notified by the W.R.A. office that I am on the cleared list and that I*

can travel anywhere in the United States including Hawaii if the Army approves the trip.

My loyalty to the United States is unquestioned and unshaken, I still sincerely believe that my internment was not justified in as much as I had been doing all I could to help those with dual citizenships to expatriate themselves. As a necessary procedure I had to write to the Japanese consulate. My family has always lived the American Way of Life. We think, live, and speak American.

We are hoping and praying that the petition will be given a favorable consideration and that permission will be granted us to return to Hawaii which we consider home. We will greatly appreciate if you would kindly notify us when the decision has been made. Thank you very much.

*Yours most sincerely,
Paul S. Osumi*

On June 7, 1945, Eugene V. Slattery, Lt. Col., J.A.C.D., legal officer of the Office of Internal Security, Iolani Palace Grounds, Honolulu, T. H., submitted a Groupings on the Return to Hawaii List to the Commanding General's Review Board. My father was No. 5, and it was recommended that he be placed on the Return to Hawaii List.

On June 13, 1945, Robert B. Griffith, Lt. Col. Infantry, wrote to my father, stating that his permission to return to Hawaiʻi had been approved by the commanding general. He wrote that as soon as transportation became available, they would make the necessary arrangements for our return.

In July 1945, the War Relocation Authority gave my family permission to travel. We left Gila Relocation Center on July 20, 1945 and moved to 2538 California Street in Denver, Colorado. This was with the assistance of Rev. Susu-Mago, who had left earlier and was already living in Denver.

Testimonies by Close Friends at the Gila Relocation Center

On April 17-18, 2008, my wife and I travelled to Puyallup, Washington in order to interview Yoshiko Yuki Yanagawa and Nobue Yuki Uchida, the two eldest daughters of the Yuki family, who had lived in the same block as my parents in Gila. The youngest daughter, Dorothy Yuki Harada, then of Oregon, had a prior commitment and was not able to meet with us.

Yoshiko wanted to forget about the internment period of her life and did not talk to her children about it. She had been a nurse, so had spent most of her time working in the hospital at Gila. She knew my father from church. She told us she had wanted Father to marry her and her fiancé, but he had come down with the valley fever and was unable to perform the ceremony. She mentioned that a man was shot for trying to leave the camp without approval, and that people committed suicide after the war broke out. Her memories of my father were that he was a very popular minister, and that he was in charge of the youth group.

The second daughter, Nobu, as I called her, said that our fathers ate at the mess hall everyday where Mr. Yuki worked. When my father became ill, her father would check on him. He told Father to see a doctor because he was not eating and was getting very ill. Mrs. Yuki took care of my father. She got his food and washed his clothes.

She said my father did not want to worry my mother and so told her little about his illness. It was Mr. Yuki who wrote to my mother and told her she should come to the relocation camp to take care of Father. According to Nobu, he was very ill and they were very concerned. They thought that he would die in the camp.

My mother was worried about taking my brother and me to Gila, but she did decide to take us with her. Her mother also influenced her decision to go to Gila.

Once we were at Gila, Father's condition improved. Nobu said you could see the changes in his expression and the happiness in his face. His face color brightened when we arrived. My mother took food to him and took care of him while Nobu and Dorothy watched over my brother and me.

I would not go to my father, because I was not familiar with him. He would not hold me at first, because he didn't want me to cry. I inched my way closer to him each day. It was some time before I would go to him and he could hold me.

Yoshiko and her husband left the camp first. When the rest of the Yuki family prepared to go, Nobu wanted to stay and finish her junior year at Gila. My parents were happy to invite her to stay with us; they always wanted a daughter, and Nobu became our calabash sister. Over the years, I did not know why Nobu always called my parents "Mother" and "Father," and my brother and me, "Brother." I felt very close to Nobu and like a brother to her.

Mother told Nobu that my father was baptized "Paul" because his given name was Sutekichi, which means "Throwaway." According to Nobu, my mother said that the government picked up Father when the war broke out because he gave sermons over the radio, probably in Japanese, and that the government felt he was giving coded messages to the Japanese Navy. In the military archive records I searched, this was not found to be true. There is no record of my father giving sermons on the radio, either in English or Japanese.

Nobu described camp conditions in great detail. There were armed military guards in towers at each corner of the camp, which was surrounded by barbed wire. There was an area between the barbed-wire fence and the camp that no one was allowed to step foot in or they would be shot. She heard that a boy was shot because he chased after a ball that went under the barbed wire.

Castor oil bean plants grew outside the barracks. Coolers with sawdust, and water running through with a blowing fan, kept down room temperatures. Gila had floors that were better than other camps, which had blacktops. The stoves burned oil, not coal, which was much better than at other camps, and the barracks had double roofing, which kept the temperature lower.

There were two shifts for people to eat at the mess hall, and there was a time limit for a person to eat and then leave. The food was terrible, she said: beans, green meat, cold baloney, moldy bread.

Outside there were coyotes, rattlesnakes, blue lizards, kangaroo mice, bats, scorpions, black widow and tarantula spiders and ugly jack rabbits with really large ears. During dust storms, everything in their room would be covered with dust.

They received $12 per month for clothing necessities, while the average person got $16 and the top person got $19. Twice a week there were outdoor movies, which cost two cents and you had to bring your own chair. There were baseball games, and there was sumo wrestling and football. The outside bathrooms had community toilets and showers.

All mail was checked and packages were opened. The Japanese people were creative, though, and built a shortwave radio to hear what was going on outside of the camp.

Nobu felt that it was not all bad—there was free food, they had a roof over their heads, and they didn't work. The *issei* ("first generation Japanese") got a rest for the first time, she said, after having worked so hard before the war started.

She remembered my father well. The camp people were impressed with his English. He was considered handsome and was very popular; girls that did not belong to the church would attend just to see Father. He kept people's interest in his sermons with light humor or jokes, even when the weather was warm and people got drowsy. He had a sense of humor that relaxed you when talking to him. Father was always a gentleman.

My father would say to Nobu that he had a "captive" congregation at his church. He conducted English sermons on Sunday mornings, and a Japanese sermon in the afternoon. There was Sunday school for the children, a choir and pianists.

He had lots of friends, both throughout the entire camp and outside. When Nobu was staying with us, Father lectured her to call her mother "Mother" and not by another name. Show respect to your mother and call her "Mother," he said. I always wondered why I called my mother "Mother." Now I know.

Osumi family with Nobue Yuki, Gila Relocation Camp (1945)

Nobu had no problem talking about the internment years with her two sons, or with others, since she believes this is history and these events happened. Pictures that we have from camp were taken by outsiders, such as visiting ministers, as no one in the camp was allowed to have a camera.

Nobu mentioned that the African-American and American-Indian people were nice to them, since they were treated in the same manner as the Japanese; they, too, endured racial prejudice and discrimination.

In 2009, Dorothy Yuki Harada wrote me a letter. She apologized that we could not get together when I was there with Nobu and Yoshiko.

She had been 11 years old when they went to Gila, and remembered my father receiving a large box of games and toys. He decided it could be a library of toys. So she and a friend started making up little cards to "check out" the toys to other children, and they had fun playing "Library."

Also, someone gave Father a black bicycle, which she learned to ride. There was a baseball field in front of his room and she would coast down the pitcher's mound. She mentioned that the bike took quite a beating and she still had scars from it.

Dorothy remembers my mother getting food from the mess hall for my father when he was ill, and she would babysit me while my mother was with him. Father baptized her one Easter morning. She wrote that my parents were wonderful people.

Final Days on the Mainland

When we lived in Denver, I was told that in front of our house was a white community, and in the back was an African-American community. My brother and I would play with the African-American children. They were very friendly with our family.

The war ended on September 2, 1945. The Gila Relocation Center closed on October 1, 1945.

Our family finally left the mainland on December 4, 1945, by ship from Wilmington, California. Four years after the start of the war, my father was finally free and he was going home with his family. He had been wrongly accused of being an enemy agent, and had been arrested, imprisoned and shipped to a prisoner-of-war camp. I am sure that when he became very ill, was lonely without his family, and was discouraged, he did not understand why all of this happened to him. I know, too, that he was frustrated by his many unanswered attempts to be released.

In a letter to a friend, he wrote that what happened to him made him a better minister. I truly believe that he felt that to be true.

I can only imagine his feelings as he woke up from a four-year nightmare and found himself starting a new life.

CHAPTER 6

Return To Hawai'i

Waialua Pilgrim Church

I believe my father was excited, happy and relieved to be returning home to Hawai'i. I am sure everything that happened to him since the start of the war, December 7, 1941, impacted his thinking, but he must have put that in the past and looked to his future as a minister in order to better serve the community. Mr. Ted Haga, a former Mid-Pacific high school classmate who lived in Waialua, asked Father to be the minister at Waialua Pilgrim Church, and he accepted. He served as the minister at Waialua Pilgrim Church (now called Waialua United Church of Christ) beginning in 1946, when he first returned to Hawai'i.

I was only four to seven years old during that period, so I do not remember much about growing up in Waialua, nor about the church where Father was minister. It was in 1947 that he wrote *God in the Desert* (one-minute sermons for devotional reading). He wrote that it was "dedicated with deep appreciation to Miss Elsie Wilcox whose unfailing friendship meant so much to us in our trials." Ruth Isabel Seabury, secretary of Missionary Education, American Board of Commissioners for Foreign Missions, Boston, Massachusetts, whom my father got to know, wrote the Introduction:

> *Many people have found real inspiration and a spiritual experience from Paul Osumi's devotional messages as they have come out in three installments in the Envelope Series. Now we present these "cactus flowers" in booklet form.*

Waialua Pilgrim Church (1946)

As pastor in a Relocation Center for Japanese Americans through the war days, Paul Osumi followed in his ministry the men who went from the Center into the U.S. Army service all over the world. The words of their pastor sustained them wherever they went. To some listening to him in the little barracks church, his words and spirit provided courage for the journey ahead into danger. For some his weekly meditations, finding them in Italy, or North Africa, gave gifts of fellowship and strength. When the war was over they asked their pastor if he still had kept those meditations. He had, and they immediately demanded that some permanent form be found for them.

When I saw the manuscript I coveted it for a wider audience. It seemed to me that in suffering and in sorrow these, our fellow citizens of Japanese origin, had experienced a degree of spiritual strength which we badly needed in the frustration and futility that many people are feeling today.

In the frayed nerves and broken spirits of this bewildering and atomic age, I believe we need the calm, serene, radiant and expectant confidence which Pastor Osumi shared with his boys to hold them strong. Here are enough to provide daily devotional material to last from New Year's Day up to the beginning of Lent, or weekly services from January through September. Separate meditations on many timely topics will fit into many types of Young People's or Adult programs.

In the hope that for many, as for me, there may be here these words of one who has kept close to God on a mountain top or in desert waste, I gladly introduce my friend, Reverend Paul S. Osumi of Hawaii.

Today's Thought: Rev. Paul S. Osumi

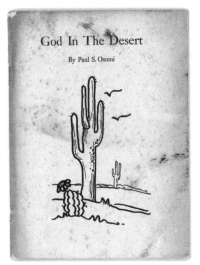

God in the Desert

Reading what Father wrote during his internment years for soldiers going off to war, I can see that he was providing daily inspirational guidance. The following are excerpts from a few of his inspirational and meditational messages, which you may have read when the *Honolulu Advertiser* was printing his daily Today's Thought:

What Do You Put First In Your Life?

When the Titanic was about to sink in the Atlantic, a wealthy woman passenger ran back to her stateroom to pick up her three oranges instead of her diamonds and other valuables. In the lifeboat oranges have priority over diamonds.

In life we are occupied with many interests and activities and we must place them in the order of their importance. We must put first things first.

How Old Are You?

What is the use of living longer if we have nothing worthwhile to live for? Life is not measured by duration but by intensity.

A character in a play says, "How tragic it is that people seem content with what is not life at all?" We ought to lay hold of something that endures and live for it.

Are You a Successful Failure?

We often make the mistake of calling ourselves "a failure" when we have not realized our ambition. An unattained ideal is not a failure. A man ought to be judged not by what he has done but what he purposed to do and tried to do.

What Are You Looking At?

Life can become mud or stars, depending on our outlook. If you have the eyes of criticism you can always find faults in everything and everybody. On the other hand, if you have the eyes of appreciation, lo, the whole world changes into the world of beauty and loveliness.

Do You Know The Secret Of Happiness?

The secret of happiness lies in one word, "sharing." Someone said, "To live is to give." Life is giving, not getting. It is a strange but true paradox of life that one gives, the more he keeps.

Are You Handicapped?

When Ole Bull, the great violinist, was giving a concert, his A string snapped and he finished it on three strings. Beethoven wrote great music although deaf. Milton was blind when he wrote poetry. Blind, deaf, and dumb, Helen Keller became a radiant soul.

Have you some handicap? Stop pitying yourself. Cease envying others.

According to Melvin and Eileen Maeshiro, high school students during my father's ministry at the Waialua Pilgrim Church, the church was always full. They said he was a "real down-to-earth" minister. The church had a youth group, called the Christian Endeavor Group, which was very active. Father would use our car to pick up youths for church activities. There were neighbor island trips, where the youth group would meet with other church youth groups on Maui and Kauaʻi. The group was called the Deputation Team, and my father would escort them. He was well-liked by church members.

I truly believe he followed his messages, since he was always there helping others. In an excerpt from a bulletin to his church members, he wrote:

"Your minister wants you to look upon him as your servant. He is your spiritual advisor. He has been trained to help people with their personal, family and business problems. Feel free to call upon him at any time. Call him when you, your loved one, or a friend is ill or going to the hospital. Notify him when there is a death in the family. He can give comfort and counsel at your difficult times. He is your minister."

In 1949, my father taught simple conversational and written Japanese (it cost $1/month to attend twice a week, plus 65 cents for the textbook). I believe he did this only because there were no other Japanese language schools, and the community wanted someone to teach the Japanese language at the Waialua Plantation.

We lived in a parsonage next to the church. Father had an office in the front of our house where people would come to see him. We had an old Plymouth that he drove us in to Honolulu when we went to do business at the church's headquarters, visit relatives, shop, eat at a restaurant or sometimes see a movie. I remember the car would travel slowly up the hill to Wahiawā, going to downtown and also coming home from Waipahu to Wahiawā. This was the same car that my father used for the church youth activities.

ʻEwa Community Church

In 1949 we moved to ʻEwa, where next my father was the minister at ʻEwa Community Church for nine years (until

Ewa Community Church (1949)

1958). I spent most of my later childhood growing-up days on the 'Ewa Plantation. 'Ewa Plantation was well maintained and I saw it as the nicest plantation in Hawai'i. I still have very good memories of the community and of my childhood friends.

The plantation's manager, James Orrick, and his wife supported my father as minister at the 'Ewa Community Church. Assistant plantation manager Ed Bryan and his wife; Ross Bachman, principal of 'Ewa Elementary and Intermediate School and many other plantation managers and community members also supported him. Besides people from the plantation, Father was able to get various military families from Barbers Point Naval Station, located next to the 'Ewa Plantation, to become active in the church.

Father learned to speak Ilocano (a Filipino language) from the plantation yardmen, who took care of the church premises. After learning the language, he conducted church sermons in Ilocano for Filipino plantation workers who were Protestants. Until then, there was no church in the 'Ewa Plantation community providing this religious service. He also started learning Chinese and Hawaiian from church members, but he did not complete learning the languages before moving on to Nuʻuanu Congregational Church.

In 1956, Father took a study tour of Christian mission stations, colleges and universities in the Pacific Rim, including Japan, Okinawa, Taiwan and the Philippines. People he visited in the Philippines were surprised that he could converse with them in Ilocano. I was told that some Filipino church members were concerned about his safety there. The war had just ended, and Filipinos in the Philippines had negative feelings toward Japanese people because of how they had been treated when Japan occupied the Philippines. Nevertheless, my father still wanted to visit the churches and other institutions.

Ed Miyake, manager of the Tenney Village Café, went fishing with my father every Monday at Barbers Point Naval Station. This was what my father enjoyed doing on his day off. He had obtained special permission from the military to fish at Barbers Point, and he and Ed would catch a few large moi, papio, ulua and oio. We always had lots of fish to eat and to this day I enjoy eating fish. Like my father, I love the ocean and fishing, and found peace and quiet in the pastime.

One day while he was fishing by himself, my father passed out on the reef. A patrolling naval military police officer found him and saved his life. He was blessed to have been saved and to be able to continue helping people until his passing.

The ʻEwa Community Church membership grew, and the church needed a larger chapel. The chapel was actually cut in half and enlarged, and you could not tell it was cut in half. A new parish hall was built in back of the chapel in 1950. Later, members of the church built additional classrooms.

My father was also active in other community organizations. He was the PTA president of the ʻEwa Elementary and Intermediate School from 1950 to 1951, and president of the ʻEwa Lions Club from 1956 to 1957.

In 1952, Congress passed the Walter-McCarran Immigration and Nationality Act, which established restrictive immigration quotas, and removed the restrictions that prohibited Asians from becoming U.S. citizens. People like my father could now become citizens. Thousands of Japan-born residents became naturalized citizens in the next years.

When I started researching his history, I had wondered why my father was not a U.S. citizen before the war. He was finally naturalized on March 26, 1953.

We left 'Ewa Plantation in 1958. My father then became the senior minister at Nu'uanu Congregational Church in Honolulu.

Nu'uanu Congregational Church

On July 1, 1958, my father was installed as the senior minister at Nu'uanu Congregational Church. This is the church where he and my mother had been married in 1933. He must have been very proud to be accepted at Nu'uanu Congregational Church.

Nu'uanu Congregational Church (1958)

Janet and Paul Osumi in front of Nuʻuanu Congregational Church

Because of limited parking, the church was relocated from its old site, at the corner of Nuʻuanu Avenue and School Street, to its present and spacious site on the Pali Highway. The new site belonged to Klebahn and Angus Estates, which covered 3-1/2 acres.

There were, I heard, some church members who did not agree with my father's leadership and left the church. Others criticized him. But he had support from other church members, and today the church still benefits from his decisions and determination.

My father is quoted in the book, *Dendo: One Hundred Years of Japanese Christians in Hawaii and the Nuʻuanu Congregational Church*, by Mary Ishii Kuramoto. At the Canvass Sunday on July 1, 1962, he said:

> *The opportunity to have a share in the building of a beautiful new sanctuary does not come often. Perhaps, it may only come once in one's lifetime. Now we have such an opportunity. This is the opportunity for us to do something for God, something that represents the biggest and best and bravest we can do—an act of dedication and sacrifice that will glorify His name.*

The new church site, at 2651 Pali Highway in beautiful Nuʻuanu Valley, conducted its first Sunday service on August 5, 1962. The new sanctuary was dedicated on November 21, 1965. An administration building was erected later.

I found in my father's files some of his achievements and recognitions while serving as minister at Nuʻuanu Congregational Church:

- Provided the invocations at the State of Hawaiʻi's House of Representatives opening in 1962, 1963 and 1964

- Elected first president of the Hawaiʻi Conference of the United Church of Christ in 1963

- Installed as moderator for the Hawaiian Evangelical Association of Congregational Churches in Hawaiʻi in June 1963

- Represented the Board of World Ministry of the United Church of Christ as one of two corporate members in June 1963 to 1967

- Named "Father of the Year in Religion" on June 9, 1963, by the Chamber of Commerce of Honolulu

- Awarded a Certificate of Appreciation and a Ceremonial Sake Cup on June 15, 1968 by the Japanese government for creating a strong Japanese foundation and for his service to the people in Hawai'i

- Gave the Benediction at the State of Hawai'i Inauguration for Governor John Burns in 1970 and 1971, and for Governor George Ariyoshi in 1974

- Spoke at numerous meetings for various organizations, companies, high schools, colleges, etc.

- Gave sermons at other churches, and speeches at special occasions, funerals, weddings and gatherings

On August 20, 1967, he traveled on a worldwide trip with my mother. They returned on November 14, 1967. I was very happy that my parents were able to travel and see the world while they were still healthy.

After Father passed away in 1996, my mother started cleaning his office and the files he kept in our home in Nu'uanu. I believe many of his awards and recognitions were discarded at that time.

It was Rev. Grant S. C. Lee, who served with my father as youth minister at Nu'uanu Congregational Church in October 1971, and then as associate minister in 1974, who wrote the letter in the introduction to this book.

Dorothy Kusumoto, who was the Nuʻuanu Congregational Church administrator during the latter years of my father's working there, said:

> *I had high respect for your father. He was a people person who every day coming to work would take the time to say 'hello' and chat with each person he came in contact with, including the groundskeeper, maintenance person, and office personnel. I never heard him yell at anyone. He said the only time to yell is when there is a fire.*

In 1988, President Ronald Reagan signed the Civil Liberties Act, providing redress to each living internee with a $20,000 cash payment. An official apology was read and signed by President Reagan in 1990. I found the following letter from The White House in my father's files, and assume that each internee received the same:

> *A monetary sum and words alone cannot restore lost years or erase painful memories; neither can they fully convey our Nation's resolve to rectify injustices and to uphold the rights of individuals. We can never fully right the wrongs of the past. But we can take a clear stand for justice and recognize that serious injustices were done to Japanese Americans during World War II.*
>
> *In enacting a law calling for restitution and offering a sincere apology, your fellow Americans, in a very real sense, renewed their traditional commitment to the ideals of freedom, equality, and justice. You and your family have our best wishes for the future.*
>
> *Sincerely,*
> *(Signed) George Bush*

Japanese Weddings in Hawai'i

In 1965, my father started doing Hawai'i weddings for couples from Japan. In his files, the first Japanese couple documented as married in Nu'uanu Congregational Church was Mr. and Mrs. H. Takagi of Tokyo, according to a letter dated May 13, 1968. My father offered a Christian wedding service to these couples from Japan. Brides wore a white wedding gown and walked down the aisle with an organist playing music. Bridegrooms wore a tuxedo. Sometimes a soloist sang.

Besides serving the mission of the Christian church, Father loved to lecture young couples about marriage and how to retain a happy marriage. The majority of the Japanese couples were not Christians, but he still wanted to talk to them. I know he married some very famous couples from Japan.

He was very busy with the weddings and my mother had to help him. The Japan weddings started to provide additional income for the church. Other churches, travel agencies and hotels started their own Japanese wedding packages, hiring taxis (limousines), flower shops, photographers, video companies, wedding gown rentals, restaurants, etc. What my father started—doing Japan weddings in Hawai'i—brought millions of dollars to the state's economy over the years. Although this did become a multi-million dollar business here in Hawai'i, I do not believe Father fully understood what he had created.

In 1993, while I was on a business trip in Orlando, Florida and staying at one of the Disney hotels, I saw a Japanese couple getting married like it was being done in Hawai'i. I was amazed that the weddings had gone as far as Florida.

Retirement

On June 30, 1974, my father retired from Nu'uanu Congregational Church as senior minister. The following year, the Honolulu City Council passed a resolution commending him for his contributions to the community. It was read by the Honolulu City Council chairman at his retirement banquet.

Nu'uanu Congregational Church called Father back to minister the Japanese-speaking congregation (Nichigobu) as an associate minister from August 1975 to January 1980. I knew he visited many older members at their homes, hospitals and nursing homes. My parents took a trip to Japan from April 5-30, 1980 after his final retirement.

Family

I remember once when Father took my son Matthew shore fishing with him. My father and my son, who was about 10 years old at the time, both loved fishing. I do not remember whether they caught any fish, but I remember Father saying that my son had a lot of patience. When Matthew's line got tangled, he sat there and untangled it, even if it took a long time.

My father had a humorous side. My daughter Koren told me that when she was helping him years later, after he had had a stroke, he told her he "liked to talk to God because God would never answer back." He also mentioned to her that he preferred living in Hawai'i when he was growing up, rather than Japan, because his family had had an arduous life in Japan and he was always picked on because he was the youngest.

There were both advantages and disadvantages in growing up the son of a minister. Friends were always cautious about what they said and did in my presence. "He is a minister's son," they would say. Many times I was identified as "PK" or "Preacher's Kid." I always felt I had to behave. During my younger years I rebelled many times.

I also met many famous and important people. My parents gave me the guidance to be the person I am today; Father never lectured me from a religious standpoint, but only did so from a father's standpoint.

Things he taught me while I was growing up:

- Take care of your health because it's one of the most important things that you have. All the money and fame in this world are not worth anything if you do not have good health. Rich and famous people are willing to give up all their wealth and fame for good health, if they have poor health. Also, good health is a God-given gift and you should take care of it.

- Family comes before work. It is not worth working long hours, day after day, week after week, month after month, year after year, only to lose your family. There are times you may be required to work long hours, but do not do so indefinitely.

- Money is not the reason for happiness. People always want more and are not happy with what they have. True and long-term happiness does not come from material things. Good health, loving family, loyal friends, positive attitude, helping others and giving more than receiving are a few things that bring happiness.

My father's words had a great impact on my life. When my daughter Koren was about five years old, I worked for a private company. There was tremendous pressure to get many large projects done on time, and over a 10-month period I was putting in more than 80 hours per week, which meant working on Saturdays and Sundays. I would leave for work before my daughter got up and return home after she was asleep. One day I was home when she was awake, and she said to me that I did not love her because I was never home.

I realized I was losing my daughter to work. The pay was very good, but I turned in my resignation the following week. My decision was made based on my father's guidance, and I never regretted it.

Many people married by my father have told me that even to this day they remember his 10 commandments for a happy marriage:

1. *Remember marriage is a 100-100 proposition. It is not a 50-50.*
2. *Neglect the whole world rather than each other.*
3. *Never meet or part without an affectionate hug or kiss.*
4. *Each day say at least one nice thing to each other.*
5. *Never go to bed angry. Settle all differences before the sun goes down.*
6. *Do not argue. Always talk things over.*
7. *Do not nag or indulge in fault-finding.*
8. *Never bring up mistakes of the past.*
9. *When you have made a mistake, say, "I am sorry," and ask for forgiveness.*
10. *Never raise your voice or shout at each other unless the house is on fire.*

They especially remember the first and last commandments.

My wife and I also had to see my father, and hear his lecture and commandments, before we got married.

When I was going out with my friends during my college years, my mother always said, "Take care and be careful." My father always told my mother, "He is old enough to know what he is doing." I believe that sometimes I was not "old enough," and that I gave my parents headaches.

My mother told me that she wished Father spent more time with my brother and me. But I understood that his ministry and the church were his first priority. He was there to help people who needed his guidance. He ministered not only to people who belonged to his church but also to all people who came to him. Even prisoners would call or write to him.

I remember that once that he got a call from someone who was going to commit suicide by jumping off the Pali Lookout. He quickly called the police and immediately left the house to go to the lookout. The person did not commit suicide. I can only imagine what Father must have said to this person.

People came to him with their problems and I believe that is why he was so determined to write Today's Thought in the *Honolulu Advertiser* for more than 35 years. People needed guidance in their lives and he tried to provide that.

My wife and children never viewed my father as a minister, but as a father-in-law and grandfather. Father made it a point each year to give both my wife and my brother's wife a Thanksgiving gift for being good wives. He was proud of his grandchildren's achievements and very supportive of them, and they also received a special gift from him each year. My brother and I would always kiddingly ask Father, "Where is our gift?"

CHAPTER 7

Today's Thought

My father wrote daily inspirational and non-denominational sayings he called Today's Thought which appeared in the *Honolulu Advertiser* six mornings a week starting in 1957. They also ran in the *Hawaii Hochi* starting in 1960, and the *Fairbanks Daily News-Miner* in Nome, Alaska from 1980 to 1984.

Over the years, family members told me that Father got many of his Today's Thought inspirational sayings from his own life experiences; from talking to people he met through his ministry; from reading the Bible, books, magazines, newspapers and letters; and sometimes by waking up in the middle of the night to write down a thought. At home, he had a very large library of books and magazines.

When he started out in his ministry as a young man, he worked with many YMCA and church youth groups, and wanted to give these young adults guidance in living a happy and meaningful life.

Many of his Today's Thought pieces were about life in general. You may say what he wrote is merely "common sense," but until people read the messages, they do not internalize them. This, I believe, is the reason that Today's Thought was the most-read article in the morning paper for daily inspiration for more than 35 years.

He received thousands of appreciation letters from people in every walk of life. Very often his inspirational messages were clipped from the newspaper, posted and saved. People told me that they have the clippings in their wallet or purse, on their refrigerator or on their mirror in their home or in their office. People say that his inspirational sayings helped them in their daily life. One person told me that Father's daily sayings gave people in Hawai'i a set of values for living happy and meaningful lives.

Lenny Yajima Andrew, former president and executive director of JCCH, wrote in that organization's July 2007 *Legacies* magazine that for years, her father, Tad Tadashi Yajima, would place a neatly folded newspaper clipping of my father's Today's Thought at the breakfast table for her to read. According to Lenny, "It was a wonderful way to start each day."

Today's Thought Books

In 1966, my father wrote and published a book called *Today's Thought* and then, subsequently, he published Volumes II and III. He dedicated the first book, available for sale on June 23, 1966, to Dr. and Mrs. Theodore Richards. Dr. Richards had been his benefactor, who enabled him to attend the University of Hawai'i.

He dedicated Volume II, published in 1994, to Mr. and Mrs. Lloyd Killiam. Lloyd Killiam, secretary of the University YMCA, had paved his way in ministry. He dedicated Volume III (1990) to U.S. Senator Spark M. Matsunaga, who devoted his life to promoting interracial understanding and world peace.

The English versions of Volume I and II were translated into Japanese books titled *One Day, One Thought* and these were also published. He gave one of the Japanese version books to each couple from Japan that he married.

As I mentioned previously, in 2006 I bought the remaining copies of all three volumes from the local publishing company, and our resulting sales of the books were great. People who bought the books told me that they still remembered my father's daily sayings. They encouraged me to write this biography and republish his daily inspirational sayings.

CHAPTER 8

Last Years of Life

My father had a stroke, his first, in June of 1993. This stroke paralyzed half his body, which took much away from his physical abilities, but his mind was still sharp and clear.

With the assistance of my daughter Koren, he continued to provide the *Honolulu Advertiser* with his daily Today's Thought column. Koren helped him gather previously printed daily sayings and she typed them for the newspaper. She and my father became very close during this time, and he told her a lot about his life that even I did not know.

Koren mentioned that a man with a donkey who was traveling around the United States had sent my father postcards from different places. This man was an educated philosopher, and my father really liked what he was saying in his postcards and got some of his inspiration from him. I did not learn his name. I found, among my father's memorabilia, a metal figurine of a prospector and a donkey, and after my daughter told me about this person I realized that it had special meaning for my father. My daughter said that this person did give Father this metal figurine, as well as a picture of himself with the donkey.

I did not find the postcards, any pictures of him or any information about this person. Nor do I know how my father knew him. After my father passed away, my mother may have discarded the postcards and the picture while cleaning.

In April 1994, the Toastmasters International District 49 honored my father as "Best-Read Author in Hawai'i" with its

Communication and Leadership Award. An excerpt from the article they wrote about him is in the introduction to this book.

Two months later, in June of 1994, my father had a second stroke. He became physically disabled and went to Maluhia Hospital, where he stayed from June 1994 to April 1996. In 1995, I took an early retirement from Bank of Hawai'i and every day I took my mother to see my father. I escorted her shopping and drove her to other places she needed to go.

I felt so sad for my father, seeing him in his disabled state. He could no longer speak or even move in bed without assistance. He had such a hard life and helped so many people. Seeing him suffer so much was very difficult for me.

Father passed away on April 8, 1996 at the age of 90. Although I was very sad to lose him, I was relieved that he was rid of all his pain and suffering, and that he had joined his spiritual Father in heaven.

Two days later, there on the front page of the *Honolulu Advertiser* at the very top, was an article by *Advertiser* staff writer Greg Wiles. It was headlined: "Hawaii's minister, Paul Osumi, dies at 90." An excerpt from this article is in the introduction.

Father's memorial service, at Nu'uanu Congregational Church, drew so many people that the church set up a video screen in its special events room so everyone could see and hear the funeral service. Although I was sad at the funeral, I was surprised and honored by the number of people who came, and by people who told me they read Today's Thought.

Among the letters and notes from dignitaries:

U.S. Senator Daniel Inouye: "Reverend Osumi will be missed by all who knew and loved him. He will live on through the wisdom and compassion he imparted on the many people whose lives he touched."

U.S. Senator Daniel K. Akaka: "He will hold a special place in our hearts as he shared his optimism *and the wisdom of the ages through Today's Thought which he authored for more than three decades. We take comfort in the thought that his legacy is everlasting."*

U.S. Representative Patsy T. Mink: "*The kindness of his spirit, wisdom of his advice, and goodness of his heart will be remembered by many who knew him personally, and many who did not have the pleasure but were touched each and every day by his 'thoughts' published in the newspaper."*

State of Hawaii Governor Benjamin J. Cayetano: "*For almost four decades, Reverend Osumi's words of wisdom and encouragement inspired thousands of readers each day through his popular Today's Thought newspaper column. Through his simple but powerful messages of advice, he was a steady spiritual guide for generations of Hawaii residents."*

State of Hawaii Senator Matthew M. Matsunaga: "*Like my father, I also enjoyed reading Today's Thought. I will miss those meaningful daily words of wisdom."*

City and County of Honolulu Mayor Jeremy Harris: "*He played a very important role in our community through his wise religious counsel which he shared with everyone in his column, Today's Thought. These daily pearls of wisdom and common sense will be missed by his large following of readers."*

United Church Board for World Ministries Executive Vice President, the Reverend Dr. David Y. Hirano: "*I remember Paul as a mentor, colleague, and a friend. When I was called to be his successor, I was privileged to follow him. He had served*

> *Nuʻuanu Congregational Church for sixteen years and led it through a mighty transition. He was due to retire and he did, but that didn't mean he quit ministering. He continued to minister. He was a great man and a wonderful pastor."*
>
> *Oahu Association of the United Church of Christ, Associate Conference Minister, Rev. Grant S. C. Lee: "We remember that he was the first Moderator of the Hawaii Conference, United Church of Christ in 1963. Moreover, we are thankful for his global ministry, especially the ministry of his daily column, Today's Thoughts. This ministry brought much healing to countless number of people who may not have had the opportunity to be touched were it not for Rev. Osumi's ministry of the written word."*

The *Honolulu Advertiser* allowed the family to continue publishing his articles in the religion section of the Saturday paper. Father's daily inspirational sayings finally came to an end when the *Advertiser* was sold and became part of the *Honolulu Star-Advertiser*.

Rev. Masayoshi Wakai told me in a November 2008 telephone conversation that Father "left a footprint in Hawaiʻi." Many others have said the same thing.

Although my father was a loving husband, father and grandfather, his life was dedicated to the Christian faith and the church, and to helping all people of different racial backgrounds, wealth, status, religion, age and health.

My wife and children saw him first as a father and grandfather, before seeing him as a minister. Father used to say he had the largest congregation in Hawaiʻi through his daily inspirational thoughts in the newspapers. They represented everybody. To this day, people still remember him from Today's Thought. "If I were to live my life again, I would still like to be a minister," my father would say.

*Family photo (1983). Center: Janet and Paul Osumi.
Clockwise from top left: Carolyn, Norman, Paul Jr., Diane,
Holly, Lisa, Matthew, Koren, Carrie*

Talk to God before you talk to man, do your daily work with sunshine on your face, be energetic but not fussy, be true to yourself, and false to no man, be loyal to principle at the cost of popularity, humor no one simply because he is rich, despise no man simply because he is poor, and leave the world a little better after your stay.

My mother passed away on August 28, 2003 and was buried with my father at Oʻahu Cemetery.

Now that I have done this research and know more about Father than I did when he was alive, I wish I could talk to him one more time. I would ask him a thousand questions.

In writing this book, I present Father's life as seen through my eyes.

In addition to learning about my father, I hope you will find that the wisdom and inspiration in this book helps you live a better and happier life, as it has many people in the past. As a son, I believe my father is happy that I have written this book and that his daily inspirational sayings will still be read and will in fact become a legacy.

Part Two

INSPIRATIONAL MESSAGES

Today's Thought

Many people have a wrong idea of success. Success is not measured by the size of a man's savings in the bank, nor the kind of house he lives in, nor the power and price of the car he drives, but the kind of man he has made of himself and the contribution he is making to society. Success is not having but being.

Rev. Paul S. Osumi,
Nuuanu Congregational Church.

Today's Thought

Someone said that a man who is selfish and self-centered is like a man living in a room surrounded by mirrors. Everywhere he turns he sees himself. He is miserable because he can see nothing beyond himself. The joy of living comes from seeking something that we know to be bigger, better, and more enduring than we are.

Rev. Paul S. Osumi,
Nuuanu Congregational Church

Inspirational Messages from Rev. Paul Osumi

The following are lengthier inspirational messages excerpted and edited from sermons delivered during my father's 44 years in ministry that began on the Big Island of Hawai'i in 1936 at Hilo Japanese Christian Church, now called Church of the Holy Cross, and concluded in 1980 at Nu'uanu Congregational Church in Honolulu. I believe the topics will appeal to readers of all walks of life. Several excerpts included here originally existed only in outline form. When the outlines were rendered more fully for this book, the original intent of the sermon's message was carefully preserved.

"Living Creatively," offered on July 12, 1936, was the first sermon I found in my father's files. It reflects his worldview found in his future sermons and in his Today's Thoughts published in the *Honolulu Advertiser*.

Living Creatively

Hilo Japanese Christian Church, 1936

During the past eight centuries, the average human life has been lengthened by 18 years. In the 16th century, average length of human life was 20 years. In 1850, it was 40. In 1870, it was 45. Today it is 58. What it will be 50 or 100 years from today nobody knows, but the fact remains that the average length of human life is being lengthened by various scientific discoveries, inventions and improved ways of living.

I believe that most people in the world are most interested in knowing how to live life intensively and creatively than in knowing how to live it longer. A friend of mine gave me a book last Christmas and on the cover of the book he quoted a sentence, "Life is not measured by duration but intensity." Some people get to be old at 18 while some keep themselves young even at 70. A few weeks ago May Robson, grand old lady of the stage and screen, celebrated her birthday anniversary. She had reached the age of 71, but what she said is remarkable: "It is wonderful to be still so young."

We have only one life to live and the greatest problem in life is how to live it intensively and creatively.

In order to live life creatively, first of all, we must have the right attitude toward life. There are two types of people in the world: the people who have the appreciative attitude toward life and the people who have the critical attitude toward life. The people who have the attitude of appreciation get more out of life than the people who have the attitude of criticism. There are some people who go about life criticizing things. We call them wranglers. If you say to them "heart," they will come right back to you with "spade." If you say "white," they will say "black." They are always ready to contradict you and disagree with you. These people are the hardest people to get along with.

Life can be made interesting and creative, or uninteresting and monotonous, depending on how we look at it.

Once there was a princess. She was very unhappy and discontented because she thought she was not pretty. One day as she was weeping and brooding over her misfortune, a good fairy came and told her that she would be all right if she did three things. First, she was to smile at every person she would meet; second, she was to look for all the beautiful things she can find; and lastly, she was to do for others all the deeds of kindness possible. She immediately began to apply herself the task of doing those three things. In the end she became so busy and happy that she forgot all about her face, and the people saw she had become the most beautiful lady in the country. An attitude of appreciation changed her whole life and, incidentally, her face too.

To live life creatively, we must live in as many areas of life as possible.

Once there was a man who made a boat trip. Evidently he was a very thrifty person. In order to economize, he ate nothing but cheese and crackers during the entire trip. At the end of the journey, he found out to his great surprise that his ticket called for three full meals a day with no extra cost. There are people who live on cheese and crackers when life provides many other things.

John Stuart Mills said that man ought to live happily as a man. Man is an animal but he is infinitely more than an animal. If man lives just to satisfy his appetites, he is no better than an animal. There are many other things besides eating we can enjoy as men. We can enjoy the fellowship of our friends, the beauty of nature, good books and magazines, good music and good movies.

There are many people in the world who live in their private world. They live in a small and limited world. We ought to live in a big world. We ought to increase the number of our interests and to enlarge the circle of our friends. We ought to seek to develop every side of our personality. Our business in life ought to be to build a well-rounded personality.

In order to live creatively we must give. Happiness depends on giving rather than on getting.

The depression is still with us. In the United States, in the midst of plenty, 12 million men walk on the streets unemployed. Why do we have the depression? Why do we have so many unemployed? There seems to be an agreement among competent economists on one point. It is selfishness, the profit motive, which brought about this depression.

When a boy was asked by his teacher what shape of the world was, he answered, "Daddy says that the world is in pretty bad shape." The world is in pretty bad shape. The nations of the world are arming to the teeth. They are spending billions of dollars for armaments. Suspicion, hatred and fear seem to be rampant all over the world. Ammunition factories are working day and night to turn out dreadful implements of destruction. Europe today presents the largest armed camp in the history of the world. Five million men are armed and ready to go to war at any time. Another 7 million men could be mobilized in 10 days. Twenty thousand airplanes are ready to start things going. The world is on the brink of a great catastrophe. Civilization is about to commit suicide. Why can't the League of Nations maintain peace in the world? Why is it ineffective? It is because the leading nations of the world joined the League for self-purposes. They joined the League to get than to give. It is preventing world peace. To live creatively, we must declare "a truce on selfishness."

To live creatively, we must devote ourselves to an idea or ideal greater than ourselves.

Once there were three stonecutters in London. They were dressing blocks of granite to be used in building St. Paul's Cathedral. A stranger happened to pass by. He looked at the men working and was struck by the different manner in which the three men worked and the difference in quality of work done. The stranger walked to the side of the first stonecutter and asked him, "What are you doing?" The stonecutter replied rather brusquely, "Don't you see, I am cutting stones?" When the stranger asked the second stonecutter the same question, his reply was: "I am trying to earn some shillings." The stranger strolled over to the side of the third stonecutter and asked him the same question. "Oh", exclaimed the stonecutter with an eager smile on his face, "I am helping build a cathedral!"

Are we living just to earn our bread and butter? Or are we living to build a life as beautiful as a cathedral? Are we living to build a better world, if you please, a world where there is no racial prejudice, where there is economic justice, where all men could be brothers and worshipping one true God?

The Mystery of Life

Hilo Japanese Christian Church, 1937

The older a man grows, the more mysterious life becomes. Sometimes we say to a youth when he grows up he will know more—not entirely true. As we grow older, sense of mystery deepens. An increasing experience of life only deepens the sense of mystery. A Harvard professor received a manuscript from one of his students with an accompanying letter—the student intends to write several books and that this was the first. He starts by saying, "I have explained the universe." It really means when he grows up, he will know less. He can never explain the universe. As we grow older and have more experience and more knowledge, we come to realize after all, we know very little about life.

In every realm, the more we know, the more the mystery grows. The popular idea that science clears up mysteries in the sense that the more science there is, the less mystery is left is not true. Modern science makes even the physical universe increasingly mysterious. Our ancient forefathers thought they lived on a flat and stationary earth and were content with simple explanations. Here we are on a planet flying 18-1/2 miles a second with the nearest star 25 trillion miles away. Today we know more about the universe, more mysterious. It was a scientist who said that after all, modern knowledge is like a bonfire at night. The bigger we build fire, the greater the area of illumination becomes and the area of darkness becomes correspondingly greater. In the fields of science, economics, politics and philosophy, more knowledge is being brought to light each year. Each generation adds more to total knowledge.

Due to scientific inventions and discoveries we have come to have a great deal of knowledge about our physical world. With scientific knowledge we can take black sticky tar and change it into perfumes, medicines and many other things.

With the aid of science we can take a single wire and send through it eight different messages at the same time.

Yes, man commands immense knowledge. But after all what is already known is a fraction. There is so much we do not know. A Greek philosopher said, "One thing I know for sure, life is full of mystery, many things we do not understand." How little we know about human life. It is a queer business, this human adventure of ours. Older one grows, queerer it becomes. Everything about it is strange from birth till death. A little child beautiful today, crippled tomorrow. Great nations rising to world power and then fall like houses of sand built by children on the shore. A great servant of the public good, blotted out while some good-for-nothing drags on his worse-than-useless life. Righteousness and rottenness. Beautiful homes and insane asylums. Glorious creative work and unemployment. Laughter of little children and hundreds burned to death in a hotel fire. Yes, it is queer. Of course, we are not always conscious of the mystery. We don't bother about it too much. We absorb ourselves in immediate tasks. But it is always there. It is the abiding background of life—ever and again something happens—great love, great tragedy, a child's birth, a friend's death. A blinding alley when man has to stop and think. Something happens and we lift our eyes to see the mystery of it.

What should be our attitude toward mystery? The first lesson to be drawn from the mysteriousness of life is distrust of dogmatism. When any man says, "I've got the whole truth," distrust the man.

That is true. Life is full of mystery and we had better be thankful. Suppose there was no mystery. That means you and I could comprehend the universe completely. That in turn would mean that universe, so thin and small, could be comprehended by little minds like ours. Thank heaven that is not true. The universe is so marvelous that our minds cannot grasp it.

Once this riddle was given: "What is it that you have never seen before, but you will see it sometime?" The answer is tomorrow. We have never seen tomorrow. We do not know what tomorrow might bring to us. We are not sure about the future. I cannot understand people who spend money and time on fortunetellers. I believe all fortunetellers cannot tell the future. But suppose they had power to know the future. It would be horrible to know the future. What a drab world it would be if there was no margin of the unknown. What an uninteresting world if we knew all that would take place in future. If there were no mystery about the future, our life would be dull as a movie seen over and over again. We do not know what is in store for us. Life is a puzzle.

But we don't have to get totally pessimistic. There is an explanation. The mystery is one of life and not of darkness. We know the explanation in bits. At present we only see the baffling reflections in a mirror, but there is an explanation. Human life is strange with its hopes and tragedies. It is a triumphant song about those abiding values of life that a man can depend on and live by gloriously—FAITH, HOPE, LOVE.

Religion does not clear up the mystery of life and does not give formula to answer all questions. What our religion does do, is give us a kind of life and power withal to sustain it so that it can be lived joyously, triumphantly in the midst of the mystery. It gives us light enough to walk by; faith and hope and love. In the center of our Christian religion is a person who faced all battlements that you and I face. Hated, deserted, crucified even. And yet through it all and above it all, lived victoriously even at the last moments of life.

We don't have to be afraid. We may meet disappointments, successes, tragedies. But no matter what happens to us, we can make our life worthwhile if we believe in God. Fishermen on the coast of Brittany when launching their boats out into the ocean used to give this prayer. In the spirit of this prayer we ought to live every day:

> **Keep me, my God; my boat it is so small**
> **Thy ocean is so wide; the storm may rage,**
> **the billows o'er me fall**
> **Oh stay thou by my side.**
> **The ocean round my barque so deep, so vast;**
> **Thy love my light will be**

When darkness reigns, no star amidst the blast;
No moonbeams o'er the sea.
Keep me, my God, and whisper, "Peace be still"
When loud the wild waves roar'
Guide my little boat in safety till at morn
    it gains the shore.
Then in the harbor calm, all storms o'er past,
No more by winds distress;
The voyage ended and the anchor cast
I reach the land of rest.

Finding Ourselves

Hilo Japanese Christian Church, 1937

We are living in an interesting era. We are living in what we call a transition period. We are being ushered into a new era. But what that new era will be, nobody knows. It may be a terrible and chaotic era when all the fine things that civilization has built up so far will be destroyed by a new and devastating world war. Or it may be an era when peace and goodwill will prevail and there will be a reduction of poverty, disease and crimes. At any rate one thing is certain—a new era is in the making.

At present there is unrest all over the world. The world is slowly recovering from the effects of the Depression, but millions of men are still unemployed. The spirit of nationalism is rampant. There are war clouds over Europe and Asia. New ideas are tried and some of the old ideas are being discarded. Social programs are being experimented. Science is rapidly mastering the physical world. The old order seems to be passing and a new order seems to be in the process of appearing. We are living in an interesting age. And we who are living in this age ought to adapt ourselves to this changing world. In other words, we ought to find ourselves.

In order to find ourselves in this age, first of all, we must have an adequate philosophy of life. We are living in days of science. Science has made us see the vastness of the universe which almost staggers our imagination. Year after year scientists are enlarging the horizons of the universe. They measure stellar distances in terms of billions or trillions of light years of space. Man becomes insignificant in such a vast universe.

A skeptic declares, "Man is a sick fly, taking a dizzy ride on a gigantic flywheel." Another asserts, "Man's life has no more meaning than that of the humblest insect which crawls from one annihilation to another." A third affirms, "Men are but tiny lumps of impure carbon and water, of complicated structure, with somewhat unusual physical and chemical properties, who crawl about a few years until they dissolved again into the elements of which they are compounded." Recently a scientist reduced the human body into chemicals and says that put together, they are worth about 98 cents.

But against this skepticism and cynicism, there is the great fact of human personality. Behind the telescope is the astronomer. Beyond the machine is the machinist. Above the system of philosophy is the philosopher. The highest values in our experience of our world are personal values. Physically man is insignificant, but he possesses the most precious thing of the whole universe—human personality endowed with intelligence and moral judgment. The ability to measure space makes man greater than space itself.

Human personality is the most wonderful fact in the universe. Personality is the thing that makes us infinite worth. In order to find ourselves in this vast universe, we must believe that personality is the most priceless thing and that it is our duty to improve our personality to the fullest extent.

To find ourselves in this world, we must do our own thinking. A recent magazine article carried a suggestive title: "Are you afraid to call your soul your own?" There are too many people who, like puppets, are moved about by somebody else. Among the exhibitions at San Diego Exposition there was a robot, a mechanical man. It can shoot a gun, obey spoken commands and do practically everything that a man can do. But one thing it cannot do—it cannot think. We are no better than robots if we do not do our own thinking. Somebody said, "Our mind is like a parachute. It does not function unless it is open." We must have our mind open and do our own thinking.

It is a tragedy that so many people try awfully hard to be somebody else. We ought to be ourselves. No two persons are exactly alike. One day standing at the corner of Broadway and 7th Street in Los Angeles, I noticed the hats of the women who passed by. They were of all imaginable shapes and kinds. I failed to find any two exactly alike. We are like women's hats. We are different. Even in twins, one can detect differences. No two persons are alike in every respect. You are you and I am I. We are all individuals and we should retain our individuality. We must be ourselves.

Again to find ourselves, we must find something greater than ourselves to which we can give loyalty. The word "worship" has come from the Latin word meaning "worth." When a man finds something greater than himself to that he gives himself, he worships in the real sense of the word.

It is said that Rudolph, who was once an idol of the screen, possessed a room with mirrors placed in all directions. A man who does not worship is like him, living in a room surrounded by mirrors. Everywhere he looks he sees himself. He can see nothing beyond himself. When a man worships, the mirrors turn into windows through which he sees something beyond himself. He sees God.

God has a plan for each one of us. Beethoven used to "see" sounds marching in columns like soldiers, executing the movements and figures of mighty symphonies. When he saw all of that in his mental picture, he felt he had to say it. He couldn't say it on paper. He couldn't say it with one instrument. He had to have a whole orchestra made up of 60, 70 or 100 instruments. And each of these instruments had to be itself. When all produced their own sounds, a mighty harmony resulted.

God is trying to make music in the world by bringing together men and women of different talents and abilities. And each one of us must play his part. Life becomes meaningful when we realize that we are instruments of God in creating a better world—a world of peace, goodwill and harmony.

To summarize, we can find ourselves in this vast universe by having a philosophy of life that the ultimate truth lies not in matter but in personality. In a world where it is so easy to let somebody else do the thinking for us, can we do our own thinking? Can we be ourselves? Can we be one with God by cooperating with him in building a new world, a world where there are economic justice, racial equality and abundant life for all?

The Imperishable Hope
Hilo Japanese Christian Church, 1938

"If a man dies, shall he live again?" This is a question that has been asked from immemorial time. Every race has asked this question. Every generation has sought the answer to this seemingly puzzling question.

Death comes to us all. We cannot escape it. When it summons, we have no choice but to follow. No insulation against death has yet been found. Death is one great experience which we all share in common. In facing the mystery of death, men have asked the perennial question, "If a man dies, shall he live again?"

Somehow we refuse to believe that death ends all. There is an eternal hunger in us for future life. There is an imperishable hope in us for immortality. The belief in life beyond is shared universally. To be sure, individuals here and there have surrendered the hope that the human race as a whole, from the most uncivilized to the most civilized, and from the most ancient men to the most modern men, believe that if a man dies, he shall live again.

Recently in France, a prehistoric man was found buried. Scientists say that he might have laid there buried for a quarter of a million years. His body had been laid with one arm bent to support his head on a pillow of flints while the other reached out to grasp a weapon of stone. Evidently he had gone out of this life well armed for the next life. His generation refused to believe that death was final. From the dawn of history men have cherished the hope of immortality.

Then, there is apparent permanency of human personality. A scientist says that the average man, weighing 150 pounds, contains enough iron to make four penny nails, enough fat to make 75 candles and a good sized piece of soap, enough phosphate to make some 8,000 boxes of matches and enough hydrogen to fill a balloon and float him off among the clouds.

In addition he contains 10 gallons of water, six teaspoonful of salt, a bowl of sugar and other chemicals elements equivalent to those found in 100 dozen eggs.

Doubtlessly all these chemical elements are found in our bodies. But there is something else in a living man. It is this something that makes the difference between a living man and a dead man. We give that something such names as life, soul, spirit and personality. Let us call it personality.

Personality is the highest value in the universe. It creates all other values in the world. All biding values of life—love, kindness, beauty, honor, truth, growth, patience, service—are personal values which have evolved as the result of friction of personality rubbing up against another personality. This universe is, to borrow Dr. Shailer Matthew's words, a "personality-producing" universe. The highest thing that this universe has created is personality. These long processes of creation have evolved higher and higher forms of life, finally reaching the climax in human personality. Is the climax to be wrecked and destroyed? Would a painter destroy his best work? Would a sculptor wreck his masterpiece? If human beings seek to preserve their best, how much more reasonable does it seems that the Creator of this purposeful world should seek to conserve the individual personalities He has created?

Our belief in future life depends upon our concept of God. If God is our Creator and Father, He is bound to care for us. We human beings are surrounded by the unfailing love of God. In the life beyond, we will still be safe with Him.

Dr. Roy Smith calls the Easter morning "the happiest morning in the history of the world." It is the happiest morning because it is on this morning our Master showed us that love is stronger than death, that death is not the end. There is larger life in the world beyond for those who believe in Him. As Christians, we rejoice in the fact that we have a Master who said, "I am the Resurrection and Life, he that believeth in me will never die."

Sympathy

Līhu'e Christian Church, 1941

We often use the word "decision." Decision means to make up one's mind. One can imagine in his own mind, but it is hard to make other people's minds your own. If we reflect a moment, we can see that many of the world's tragedies occur because of the fact that we do not make other people's mind our own. Sympathy means to make someone else's mind our own. Because of the lack of sympathy we have quarrels, misunderstanding, jealousy and hatred. In order to get on in the world, we need to have sympathy.

In order to make other's mind our own, we must put ourselves in other people's places. "He who lives in a glass house should not throw stones at his neighbors." Many people in the world do not try to see things from other people's point of view. They only look at things from their own viewpoints. In order to avoid misunderstanding we do well to look at things with other people's eyes rather than with our own.

There is a barrier between the living and the dead. But even among the living, there often exists am impassable barrier. Sometimes we find among the members of a family living under the same roof a barrier, which keeps them distant.

On the other hand, it is possible to have one mind though living far apart. Spiritual intercourse transcends distance of space. There can be a unity of mind through living apart and a separation of mind through living together.

No organization can run amicably without sympathy. Home is an example. If there is to be happiness in a home, all members in that home must have sympathy with each other. Each must be considerate of others and must always think of the welfare of the entire family rather than his own. At present in the Japanese home there is nothing more important than the understanding between the children and the parents. The parents who were reared in Japan tend to run things in Japanese ways while their children who were raised in Hawai'i want to do things in American ways. This often results in conflicts and even tragedies at times. Parents would say, "I wonder why my children are disobedient?" Children would blame their parents by saying, "My parents are hardheaded and unreasonable." To retain peace and happiness in the home, the parents must see things with the eyes of the children and the children must look at things with the parents' eyes. They must not look at things from their own viewpoints.

Recently the relation between employers and employees has not always been peaceful. There have been strikes here and there. Why do we have strikes? I believe the main cause is the lack of understanding between the employees and the employers. The employees do not try to see things from the employers' point of view and the employers do not attempt to look at things from the employees' view point. It is important that we see things through other people's eyes.

Thomas Mott Osborne was a millionaire and held a high position in society. He had a deep sympathy for all the inmates of prisons. In order to know for himself the actual conditions in prisons, he entered the Auburn prison in New York as an inmate. He ate the same things the other prisoners ate and lived as they did. He lived in the prison for several years. In the Auburn prison there was a man who had committed a great crime and who looked at society and others as his foes. He was bitter and sour at the world. But when he saw Mr. Osborne living the life of an inmate because of his deep sympathy for the prisoners, he gradually began to see that there are some people in the world who were interested in him. He shed tears and became a changed man.

Sometimes there exists an invisible barrier between people, which is stronger than iron bars of the prison, and makes it impossible for them to associate with each other. What is the barrier? It is jealousy, hatred, misunderstanding and prejudice. All of this results from the lack of sympathy.

Father Damien sympathized with the lepers on Molokai and served them for many years. Later he became a leper himself. He sacrificed his life. David Livingston, because of his deep sympathy for the natives in Africa, offered his life for their service. Florence Nightingale sympathized with the wounded soldiers in the Crimean War and gave her life in nursing them. Dr. Toyohiko Kagawa, out of his deep sympathy for the underprivileged in the slums, spent many years in the slums of Kobe, ministering to the needs of the unfortunate.

We often hear about the want of material goods. But for us human beings, the lack of sympathy is greater than the lack of material goods. We can endure the want of goods but we cannot endure the want of human sympathy. The lack of sympathy between nations, groups and individuals, misunderstanding, hatred, jealousy and prejudices are rampant. The world is getting to be chaotic and dark.

We must nurture sympathy with each other and must learn to look at things from other people's point of view.

The Nurture of the Soul

Līhuʻe Christian Church, 1941

In my visit to Honolulu in July (1941), I was surprised to see a complete change in the city. Honolulu seems to be in a boom due to the influence of the defense work. Not wanting to miss the opportunity to make money, people are rushing to Honolulu from other islands. In addition, many are coming from the mainland, United States. As the result, the population of the city has greatly increased in the past year. And I noticed a great increase in the number of cars on the streets.

Honolulu used to possess an atmosphere of serenity and calm, befitting the capital of the Paradise of the Pacific. But that atmosphere seems to have gone and Honolulu is now a noisy boom town. As a result, the people are now living in a fast life.

When I saw the way the people are living in the city, I was struck with the necessity of recovering our serenity and calmness. When our body is tired, we take food to increase its vitality. Our spirit is no different from our body. We must not let it starve. We must constantly give it food. When we are living a fast life, we usually neglect to take the spiritual food. I know it is hard for people in Honolulu to take their spiritual food because they are living in noisy and confused surroundings. As the world becomes more and more civilized, the speed of life becomes faster. In olden days the people used to walk to go to any place, but nowadays we depend on automobiles. We are living in the days of speed. In doing anything, we want to get it done as soon as possible. We want to save as much time as we can. As speed of life increases, the noise of the world also increases. The sound of the automobiles passing by, the tooting of horns, passing of streetcars and trains, the noise of the airplane propellers, the sound of the telephone bells and music from the radio—all contribute to the din of the world.

We do well to get away from the unnatural noise of the world. We do well to slacken the pace of life. We must learn to keep silent and calm. The root of life withers when we are constantly and busily engaged in activities. We must get away from the confusion and noise of the world and keep silent for 10 minutes or even five minutes. To do so will be to nurture our soul. When one practices this, his body becomes strong and his mind clear.

According to the magazine, *Jtsugyo-No-Nihon*, Health-By-Sit-Breathe-According-To-Okada is very popular in Japan. Many people were cured of their sickness after having practiced this health improvement exercise. The way to do it is very simple. First, one is to sit up straight, then shut his eyes, calm himself and take a deep breath. I believe this is an effective way to improve one's health.

Two years ago when I visited London, England, I was quite surprised to see the city quiet and hushed on Sunday. Stores and firms were all closed on Sunday. There were fewer buses than usual and there weren't very many people on the streets. For six days the city buzzes with activity, but Sunday is a holiday and quietness reigns. When the surroundings are thus made quiet, the people are given the opportunity to think quietly and to improve their mind and body. I believe the reason why the British people are tenacious and strong is that they always nurture their souls.

When one neglects to cultivate his spirit due to his busyness, his inner strength is gone. Busier we become, harder we must try to keep quiet. Anybody can learn to keep quiet. "I am too busy. My business takes all my time. It is impossible to find time for meditation," some may say. But to meditate for even 10 minutes or five minutes daily is the most important thing in life and one should not neglect it. If one has the will to do it, he can. Spending five or 10 minutes in quiet meditation after one gets up in the morning is not hard. It doesn't have to be in the morning. When the day's work is done or just before going to bed, one can spend a little time in meditation. Carlyle once said, "The bee does not make honey except in darkness. Mind gives no worthwhile thought except in meditation."

There is a boarding school in the United States that makes the students keep quiet at a designated time every day when the bell rings. As a means to build the character of children, the schools in Hawaiʻi ought to set aside three or five minutes before school starts, in letting the students keep quiet. Someone said, "Words are silver, but silence is golden." Studies are important, but silence is more important.

"Know thyself. It is the supreme wisdom," said a wise man in Greece. One cannot know himself if he does not find time to sit quietly and to reflect calmly. One has conquered himself when he can sit quietly in a room and can suppress his self-will and selfish thoughts.

When we live in noisy surroundings or when we keep ourselves too busy, our inner life is affected and become dry and withered. We must find time every day to sit quietly, to calm our soul and to pray to God for strength. Then and only then can we cultivate a healthy mind.

Living Without Complaint
Līhu'e Christian Church, 1941

There are many people in the world who are dissatisfied with life. They do not find life to their liking. They are full of complaints. They think that the world is unfair to them. They would say, "Look at the other people. They are living happily and without want. Why is it that I am so unfortunate? Why didn't God make it so that all people would have an equal amount of happiness in life?" They do not realize that other people's yard always looks green when seen from their own yard. Ask the man who is known as a perpetually happy man, you would find out that he too has complaints of his own.

Once there was an old man who was known in the neighborhood as a very happy man. Having lost his wife and children, he was living alone but he was always happy. A friend asked him, "Were you ever in all your life glum and discontented?" The old man said, "Yes, once I was plumb down in the month. But I got cured right off, and I ain't ever had an attack of the blues since then. I hadn't any shoes to my name and I didn't see how I was going to manage to get a pair of shoes before winter set in. Then one day I saw a man that didn't have any feet. I can't rightly say as I've ever been discontented since then."

If a man thinks that there isn't any man more unfortunate than he is and pities and envies others, he shall never escape unhappiness. Happiness does not depend on one's circumstances or conditions, it depends on the way he manages himself. There are many people in the world who are unhappy and discontented though they possess money and possessions in abundance.

Once there were three men who went on a journey to Goshu. On the way one day, they got extremely hungry. Presently they came to an old, dingy restaurant. Upon entering it they said to an old woman who was in charge, "We don't want any tea or any other things. Get us bowls of rice." The woman replied, "All that I have is yesterday's rice." They said in unison, "We don't care whether it is yesterday's rice. We don't care how old it is. Bring it as soon as you can." When the rice was brought to them the three men greedily devoured a bowl of rice each in an instant. There was no complaint at the beginning but when they have finished the first bowl of rice, they said, "Bring something besides rice. How about bean curds?" After they have finished the second bowl, they complained, "Say lady, we hear that there is a lake nearby. Don't you have some fish?" After the third bowl they said, "This rice doesn't taste as good as it is supposed to." After the fourth bowl, their complaint was, "Why don't you keep this place clean? These bowls are too dirty."

There is no limit to man's greediness. As one becomes well off, his want grows larger. You can't say that man's greediness is as high as a mountain. There is a top and a limit to any mountain, but there is no limit in man's greediness.

How can we, then, do away with complaints? There is only one way to get rid of it. One must alter his way of looking at life. One must realize that after all true happiness does not come from things outside of us such as money, possessions, health, position or fame. In a way it is good to be bearing some burdens of life. When you have nothing to worry about, nothing to strive for, then you will most probably start complaining about life. Human beings are really funny. When they have everything they want, then they begin to "squawk."

It is the worries, hardships and difficulties that make life worth living. In the Bible, we find the following saying: "Do all things without murmurings and questionings." Let us be content with our own lot and with the help of God, live a truly happy life.

The Eyes of the Heart
Līhuʻe Christian Church, 1941

Though we live in the same world, it appears different to us depending on how we take it and how we look at it. We often say that we are glad or we are sad, we are happy or we are unhappy. What makes us feel as we do? It is not the things outside of us but the way we turn the eyes of our heart that is responsible for our moods. There are two worlds: the outside world and the inner world. And we can manage the world outside of us by the way we manage the world within us. The most important thing in the world is our heart. The thing that makes us happy or unhappy during the lifespan of 50 years is the way we turn the eyes of the heart.

Once there was a queen, who one day called two of her pages and said to one, "Go and find all the weeds in the country." And to the other she said, "Go and find all the flowers in the country." The two went as they had been told. About two or three months later they returned with their reports. One said, "Queen, it is terrible. I warn you. Your country is full of weeds." The other page said, "Queen, be glad and rejoice. Your country is full of beautiful flowers." The two men traveled the same country but brought back different reports. They had different ways of looking at things.

The man who is happy feels happy when he sees anything. But the man who is unhappy feels unhappy when he looks at the world about him. The thing to do is to change the pupils of one's eyes. Then all that is reflected as sadness will turn to gladness. The question is what to do with our eyes, whether to turn them to the right or left.

God has given to us this marvelous thing—the heart. We must know it, understand it and be able to utilize it. If we do, the whole world will change as the results. There are some people who pity themselves by saying, "I wonder why I am so poor and unfortunate. This is really a hard world." They spend their days in tears and in complaints. Those people have not yet opened the eyes of the heart that God has given them. The treasure of heart becomes useless to them.

Once there were two buckets at a certain well. They were conversing. One said to the other, "Say, you look sad. What is the matter?" The other replied, "You see, it is this way. When I go back from the well, I am full of water but when I come back to this well, I am always empty. I am sad because I always come back here empty, which shows that my work is useless." Then the other said, "You are wrong in your thinking. As for me, I come back here empty but when I go back, I am always full of water. When I think this, I am really happy. You must correct your thinking."

This is just a parable, but how true it is with people. Those who look at the dark side of life think that they are the most miserable people in the world. On the other hand, those who look at the bright side of life, think that there are no happier people than them.

Since all of us have to live in this world, why not live cheerfully? It takes 64 muscles of the face in order to frown and only 13 muscles to smile. This shows how easy it is to smile. Why not smile?

Let us turn our hearts toward the right direction and look at the good in life. Let us be pleasant. Let us recognize that there is happiness in misfortunes. At times we ought to be thankful for adverse circumstances. Even in the storms of life, let us keep our heart as clear as the blue sky. A good artisan does not throw away what seems to others as useless bits of wood. He utilizes them to make fine things. A skillful cook does not throw away leftovers. He prepares nice delicacies out of them. Even though we may be in an unfortunate circumstance, we can live happily by turning the eyes of the heart in the right direction.

Life Worth Living?

Canal Church—Gila Relocation Camp, 1943 to 1945

Some people find life worth living, while some find it quite uninteresting and monotonous and do not see how life can be worth living. What makes people see life differently? I believe it is something in them, the attitude they have toward life that makes people see life differently. Once two men walked in a rose garden, one saw beautiful roses and the other saw nothing but thorns. They went in the same garden. One saw beauty and the other ugliness. It is not what life brings to us, but what we bring to life that makes life worth living.

We often make the mistake of thinking that life is worth living for the people who are prosperous, fortunate and wealthy, and that it is not worth living for the people who are poor, stricken and handicapped.

Nobody finds life worth living; one always has to make it worth living. All the people to whom life has been abundantly worth living have made it so by the inner spiritual contribution of their own, and such people commonly are not in a fortunate circumstance. When a man thinks that life is not worth living he usually seeks escape and commits suicide. According to a statistical study of suicides made recently, there are more cases of suicide among the wealthy and fortunate than among the poor and unfortunate. The poor beggar holds onto life while the millionaire whose fortunate has collapsed, destroys himself.

There was a king in Persia who found life extremely uninteresting. With all that a king could have, material wealth and possessions, he was not happy. One day, he consulted his wise men that told him that if he could wear the shirt of a perfectly happy man, he would be all right. So the king sent his men to find the shirt of a happy man. The men hunted and searched among the aristocrats and wealthy people of the kingdom, but never found a perfectly happy man. At last they learned that there was a man who was perfectly happy and he was a laborer. They found the man but he was so poor that he did not even own a shirt. It is not something without, but something within that makes life worth living.

When life brings us hardships, difficulties and misfortunes, we tend to blame them on fate. We are apt to say, "Life is hard and cruel to me. Fate is against me." We begin to pity ourselves. But we must always remember that whenever we are in trouble we are free to do something about it. We can make almost anything work together for good.

Life sometimes seems to us extremely impartial. In the Bible we find these words, *"All things come alike to all; there is one event to the righteous and to the wicked."* All things come alike to all. A shipwreck drowns the good and the evil alike. A hurricane wrecks a village, and churches and schools are not spared. An economic disaster falls on the honest and the crook. Death visits a good man as well as a bad man. All things come alike to all.

So we conclude that it is not something without, but something within that makes life worth living. We can turn misfortunes by our inner attitude. All things will happen to us; life and death, joy and sorrow, romance and loss, friendship and bereavement, happiness and tragedy. But the outcome will depend on what we have in us. It is not what life brings to us, but what we bring to life that makes life worth living.

Spirit of Adventure

Canal Church—Gila Relocation Camp, 1943 to 1945

We live in a changing world. We are not living in a static world, but a dynamic world. We are living in a changing, developing and becoming world. Somebody said, "There is nothing permanent in the world except changes." Even our bodies change completely every seven years. New cells are formed to take the place of the cells that are used up to form a new body in seven years.

At the time of Columbus the people thought that this world was a static world. They thought that it was flat with four corners. When Columbus came forth with the new and seemly impossible idea that this world was round, the people laughed at him. In spite of severe criticisms and oppositions he finally managed to get a ship and venture out into the unknown sea. With dauntless courage and adventurous spirit he sailed on and discovered a new world.

Today nobody doubts the fact the world is a sphere moving around the sun. Today we know that the whole universe is moving. Believe or not, even the table I am writing on is alive and moving. It is made up of atoms and electrons, which are darting back and forth at an unbelievable speed.

Change is the law of life. Everything changes in the universe. So we ought to fit ourselves in this changing world. We too ought to change and develop and grow. But the tragedy of it all is that many people are afraid of change. They are afraid of new ideas and are suspicious of new experiments. If anybody comes forth with a new idea or proposal they immediately brand him as a radical.

Sometime ago in Los Angeles, a man whose name was Safety First was brought to a court for violating some traffic regulations. Evidently this man did not live up to his name. There are many people whose motto seems to be "Safety first." They say, "Play safe. Don't change anything. Keep things as they are. Keep them *status quo*."

We must have the spirit of adventure in every phase of life. Civilization is nothing but a series of changes. Tennyson said, "Men's thoughts are widened with the process of the sun." Many scientific discoveries and inventions have been made by men and women who possessed the spirit of adventure.

Pasteur, in spite of his paralysis, devoted his life to discovering the secret of a disease. Magellan, wanting to discover a new truth about the globe, started out on his perilous journey around the world. About 60 years ago, the people laughed at George Pullman for his seemingly fantastic idea that beds could be installed in railroad cars. About 100 years ago, the people jeered at Fulton for the crazy idea he entertained that the boat could be propelled by steam. Hideo Noguchi, a Japanese scientist, gave his life in Africa so that humanity could be freed from the curse of yellow fever.

Just as we need the spirit of adventure in other fields of life, we need it in our religion. We need to make our religion a dynamic religion. In the history of Christian religion there have been many who had the spirit of adventure.

Living as we are in this changing and developing world, we should never be satisfied with the existing order of things. We should always strive for something better and finer. Let us have the passion for growth and improvements. Let us have the spirit of adventure.

Being on Top of the World

Canal Church—Gila Relocation Camp, 1943 to 1945

I believe our major problem in life is how to overcome our life. You and I are after a truly happy life. In a figurative language, you and I want above anything else to be "on top of the world." But the sad thing is that that is where we seldom are. We often find ourselves burdened with cares and troubles. Outer circumstances of life whip and crush us. Here in the relocation camp we see many people who are being frustrated, dissatisfied and dejected. The Christian religion is a religion of triumph. It ought to make a man sit on top of the world. If it doesn't, then something must be the matter with his religion. His religion is not functioning.

Here is a man who says, "I am 74 years of age, and I find myself utterly unable to explain the following situations. Some years ago my wife, sick with melancholia, took her own life. Then my oldest son died of a fever. Not very long after that my oldest daughter shot herself during a mental depression. A few years later my only living son and his two small children were burned to death in their own homes. My question about life can be summarized in the single word: WHY?" Yes, it is difficult to harmonize the tragedies of life with the goodness of God. There are many things in life we do not and cannot understand.

When one has a living faith, the center of his life moves into an area that is not at the mercy of the world. When a man is primarily after wealth, he will someday be disappointed. When a man is mainly after pleasures, he will someday find life empty. But when a man's sole purpose in life is to grow in favor with God and man, then nothing will discourage him. When a man's controlling passion is to follow God's way of life, then he can capitalize anything life does to him. He can be on top of the world.

It is said that when they first made Ivory soap they were horrified because it floated on the water. They didn't want it to float. Who would buy soap that is light—so light that it floats on water? They were defeated and thought that the whole experiment had ended in a dismal failure until someone spoke up, "Let us capitalize our deficiency. Let us tell the world that it floats. Let us take a plus-attitude toward it. Let us say it floats until everybody on earth has heard it." This they did and succeeded.

Faith does not only mean believing a number of propositions. It is not credulity. It is creative power. It is a dynamic force that enables man to stand in the face of an overwhelming odd, to capitalize a deficiency, to overcome a wrong such as on one done to us by an undiscouraged spirit of goodwill. Kirsop Lake said, "Faith is not belief in spite of evidence, but life in scorn of consequences, a courageous trust in the great purpose of all things and a pressing forward to find the work which is in sight whatever the price may be."

Men of faith can do wonders. All things are possible with them. When the present diabolical, devilish, bloody business of war is over, it is only the men of faith who can rebuild the world and establish a just and durable peace. Science and inventions have made isolation impossible. They have made our world a neighborhood. We must make it a brotherhood. Our global war must be followed by a global peace.

It is only men of faith who can conquer themselves and conquer the world; men who have incarnated in themselves the words of the Master who said, "*I have overcome the world.*"

The Secret of Not Losing Heart

Canal Church—Gila Relocation Camp, 1943 to 1945

George Shaw once said, "If the other planets are inhabited, the earth is their lunatic asylum." Yes, our world seems like an insane asylum, especially at the present moment. Mankind has lost its direction, and chaos and confusion reigns everywhere. But whether we like it or not, we are living in this world and we must make the most of our lives here.

Too many people are spiritually defeated today. Too many people are getting cynical and skeptical. Too many people are finding life futile, meaningless and empty. They are crushed by the burdens of tragedy and sorrows of this war-torn world. Can we find a philosophy of life that is adequate for the desperate days in which we live?

Some scientists are saying that the sun is cooling off gradually, and that someday we shall all be dead and there will be nothing left but a burned-out cinder of a planet. Is the world coming to a dead end? Materialism says that nothing in the universe lasts and that all is transitory and will pass away eventually. Someone said, "The world cosmos is a gigantic accident consequent upon an infinite succession of happy flukes." Can we believe that? We have tried but we cannot. The difficulty with this view is that it not only runs against our wishes, but it runs against the facts of life. The more we have found out about our universe, the more wonderful and marvelous it has turned out to be. It is a paradox of life that the more we know, the less we know. The more we know about the universe, the wider becomes the area of the unknown. Due to new astronomy, Einstein's theory of relativity and quantum physics, a great store of knowledge has been disclosed. We are just beginning to find out about the universe in which we live.

According to materialism, everything is coming to an end. Everything begins nowhere and comes out nowhere. But we Christians believe that something abides and comes out somewhere, and that eternal element is in people. We believe that we live in two worlds: one visible, tangible and temporal, and the other invisible, intangible and eternal.

We believe that behind the universe is God. We often hear people deride faith in God by saying they can't believe in God because they can't see Him. They claim that since God is invisible he is unreal. No man has seen God at any time. No man has seen a thought, but thoughts are creative forces in human life. No man has seen faith and courage. In fact no man has seen himself. Yes, you can see your body, but it is not the essential part of you. The real you, you have not seen and you cannot see.

Eternal life is a quality of life so meaningful, so radiant and so joyful that it is worth continuing through the ages. Sir Wilfred Grenfell said, "I am very much in love with life. I want all I can get of it. I want more of it, after the incident called death, if there is any to be had." How alive are you in mind, spirit and in fellowship with God? There are many dead people walking on the streets. To them, the material things of life are the only reality. They live merely to satisfy their animal appetites. The tragedy of it is that they are dead and don't know it.

We are living in dark and troublesome days. Nothing will make us lose our heart if we keep our eyes on God. ✤

What is Your Average?
Waialua Pilgrim Church, 1947

Talking about average reminds me of a story. A minister was about to get off from his first ride in a Pullman. "What is the average tip?" he asked the porter. "One dollar," said the porter. The pastor gave him a dollar. Then the porter said, "Thank you, sir. You are the first to ever come up to the average."

It is said that life is a series of ups and downs. Life doesn't stay the same all the time. A spiritual says, "Sometimes I am up, sometimes I am down."

Yes, it is true that we are up sometimes and we are down sometimes. Sometimes we are on top of the world, so to speak. Everything goes on smoothly and fortune smiles on us. But at other times we are down in the valley of despondency and despair. Life gives us a hard blow and we are down. Perhaps a misfortune visits us all of a sudden and we find ourselves in grief and sorrow.

Some time ago, I received a letter from a young man in which he said, "Rev. Osumi, my life has been a series of downs." I know life for the young man had been pretty tough. But I also know that he has had moments of joy and happiness. Life doesn't travel on a smooth road all the time. It has detours. It has rough places at times.

Some years ago, there was a cartoon in one of the large metropolitan newspapers. It depicted a typical modern American business man. In the cartoon, we see the man out on the edge of a stream, fishing. He has caught a number of fish. Typical of all fishermen, he has hung his catch on a high pole in a conspicuous place where he can proudly look at them. The fish he caught in 1959 is of a fair size. The one he caught in 1936 is larger. In 1950, still larger. The 1961 fish is almost the size of a young whale, but the 1962 catch is the smallest fish of them all. And in 1963, when we see him in the cartoon, he is just on the point of pulling a turtle out of the water. The poor man's expression is one of disgust, anger and disillusionment. His hat is flying off into the air. He is trying desperately to free his line from that measly turtle.

The whole point of the cartoon is to emphasize the fact that that man's attitude toward life is wrong. He lacks perspective. His whole attention is fixed upon the measly turtle he is catching in 1963. He is so shortsighted that he cannot look back and see the splendid fish he caught the years before. He is intended to represent the spirit and attitude of multitudes of people at the present hour. I like fishing. Sometimes I come home without any fish but the average is not bad.

In order to keep a balanced attitude toward life, you must balance the good with the bad, with your eye fixed on the average.

In 1929, when stock prices were toppling and many people were losing a lot of money, two men whose fortunes on paper had shrunk thousands of dollars, looked back across the years and concluded, "Even at present prices, we are worth 10 times as much as we were 10 years ago; and if that is so, our average for the 10 years is mighty good. What are we complaining about?"

We must have a sense of perspective and a balanced attitude toward life. We must have the ability to take the long look. We must have the habit of balancing the good with the bad. We must discover the average and keep our attention upon it rather than upon the greatest gains or our greatest losses. We must keep our eyes fixed not upon just the best or just the worst, but upon the average somewhere between the good and the bad. This is the only way to keep our feet on the ground. Sometimes we get terribly upset because of the criticism we hear about ourselves. Sometimes we get highly elated and think too much of ourselves when other people praise us. "Rev. Osumi that was a very good sermon!" The best way to take praise or criticism is to cut them in half and take the average.

A young man sets out in life to sell cash registers. He made up his mind that if he could sell them to a large department store, he would have made a real success. If that great department store bought the cash registers, other smaller stores would buy them too. The first time he called upon the department store, he received neither an order nor any encouragement. He called upon the store the next year and the next and the next until finally in the 10th year, he came away with an order for $150,000. That young man had a balanced attitude toward life. He looked back over the years and said to himself, "Fifteen thousand for each year is not a bad average after all."

This attitude of balancing life is valuable not only in the business world. It is actually the way of facing life. Life has a way of balancing itself for you. Life brings both the best and the worst. When you live to a ripe old age, I am sure you can look back across the years and become grateful that you life has averaged up so well.

You know, I am still young in years, though my wife reminds me I am getting old with white hair, but I have learned one thing in life that I would like to pass on to you this morning. If you expect all your years to be equally good, you will be disappointed. You may go on for a time without getting ahead, but if, at the end of each year, you have a little more of this world's goods and a better understanding of life, be satisfied. Then there may come a year when fortune will smile upon you and you will make a lot of progress. You must expect to balance the good with the bad. Life is a series of ups and downs. When you are down, don't get terribly upset. If you have the stuff in you, you will be up again.

So, in your life, there are weak moments that bring your average down, but there are also great moments, which bring your average up. At 40, Henry Ford was in debt. He had not saved a cent. At 45, Lincoln was a disappointed politician. His friends feared that he might take his own life in a fit of melancholy. At 25 years of age, Charles Darwin worked day and night without the slightest recognition. But for Darwin, for Lincoln, for Ford, came great moments compensating for the rest. So, it will be with you.

I would like to point out briefly three things by which we can develop a balanced attitude toward life:

1. In the first place, to develop a balanced attitude toward life, we must take a long look back. What seemed a failure to you yesterday has become, with the passing of time, a triumph. What at one moment seemed to be a defeat, turned out to be a success. What once looked to you like a great loss, turned out to be a great gain. John Bunyan was within prison walls, yet, out of that loss of freedom, he wrote himself into immortal liberty in his *Pilgrim's Progress.* John Milton was stricken blind, yet in his darkness, he wrote the immortal, *Paradise Lost* and *Paradise Regained.* Dante was exiled from his beloved city of Florence. He was a wandering refugee over the face of Italy, never eating bread he could call his own, yet in those days, months and years of anguish, he wrote his *Divine Comedy* which is universally recognized as one of the greatest epics of the soul, written in any language, ancient or modern. I spent several years in a relocation center. We had to live a restricted life. We didn't have enough to eat. We had to live in barracks. Even our church was a barrack building. Pews were made of scrap lumber as well as the altar, pulpit, lectern. Only one store in the entire camp. Not many things in it. Not much money to buy them. But, looking back over the years, I can truthfully say that those were the best years of my life. The biggest congregation I ever had and will have in the future, 400 enthusiastic young people. Religion meant something to them. Shake hands with them with one hand and one hand holding a handkerchief to wipe off perspiration.

2. In the second place, to develop a balanced attitude toward life, we must take a long look around us. We sometimes tend to envy other people for what they have and what they are. We sometimes tend to think that life has been more unkind and unjust to us than it has been to other people. But if we take a long look around us, we will discover that what life brings to us is as good as what it has given to 99 out of every 100 people.

When we are tempted to indulge in self-pity, we ought to remember that our life could be far worse than it is. The Scotchman revealed a far better attitude than the Englishman in their shipwreck experience. By the end of the second week, their clothes were in tatters, their food exhausted and the outlook was dark indeed. The Englishman moaned, "It just couldn't be worse." "Ah, but it could," replied the Scotchman, "I might have bought a return ticket." Socrates was right when he said that if you could gather together all the troubles of all the people in the world, weigh them and find the average, you would pick up your own and sneak off better contented with your lot. That is what Fanny Crosby did. She was stricken blind at the age of six, yet she developed a balanced attitude toward life by taking a long look around. She saw that although she was blind, she had many things which other people did not have. Listen to her: "O what a happy child I am, although I cannot see; I am resolved that in this world, contented I will be. How many blessings I enjoy, that other people don't; to weep and sigh because I'm blind, I cannot and I won't do!"

3. In the third place, to develop a balanced attitude toward life, we must take a long look ahead. When you take a long look ahead, you inevitably look at the present moment in a totally different perspective. If you know that in the past, an apparent failure has turned out to be a victory, you live in the hope that what happened yesterday can happen tomorrow. Then you live your present moment, whatever it may be, in the faith that it is filled with unforeseen and unforeseeable possibilities. There was a young man who began his high school career determined to win the highest honor his school could offer. He worked hard with this goal in view. At the end of his high school, he had made the highest scholastic record ever achieved in that school. However, the honor did not go to him. It went to another. There

was a ruling that the first honor could not go to anyone who lived outside the city limits. He was not a resident of the city. For a time, he felt that his four years in high school had been a total failure. It was his first contact with the world, it had treated him unjustly. He went away to college under the shadow of that disillusionment. Then one day, the thought flashed into his mind that these four high school years were not the end, but only the beginning. He had all the years ahead to win what he seemingly had lost in his youth.

New courage and faith will come to you when you have enough perspective and balance to see your present moment never as the end, but as the beginning. I believe that it takes another world to finish what we have begun here. Isaac Pitman is remembered chiefly for the lasting contribution he made to the art of stenography. Many people do not know that he was also a lecturer, an astronomer, a temperance worker and a preacher. He was knighted at the hand of Queen Victoria. Pitman considered his employments as belonging not to a time, but to eternity. Shortly before his death, he gave this message to a friend, as the secret of his poised and peaceful life. To those who ask how Isaac Pitman passed away, say "Peacefully, and with no more concern than in passing from one room to another to take up some further employment." To develop a balanced attitude, we must take a long look ahead.

Making the Most of Ordinary Abilities

Waialua Pilgrim Church, 1948

I know I am not a great preacher, though I always aspire to be one. I know I am not a genius. I am an ordinary man. When I say that most of you are also ordinary people, I am sure no one will stand up and protest and say, "Rev. Osumi, you are wrong. I am not an ordinary person. I am a genius." There is nothing wrong about being ordinary. There is nothing wrong about being a part of the common masses that make up the world. Lincoln once said, "God must love common people, he made so many of them." Millions of common, ordinary men and women like you and I "make the world go round," turn the wheels of industry, till the soil, harvest the crops and build our homes. Geniuses are few and far between, and they would be useless if they did not have us common people to furnish a demand for what they have to offer.

Sometimes we begin life fancying we are gifted with unusual ability. When we are young (usually high school days), we entertain great ambitions. We cherish high ideals. We build castles in the air. We say, "Someday I will startle the world with my achievements. I will make a magnificent contribution to the world." This attitude changes by middle-age or even earlier. Our castles in the air disappear and we are driven to the conclusion that after all, we are only ordinary people.

A parable of human life is depicted in the following verses:

> A fox looked at his shadow at sunrise and said,
> "I will have a camel for lunch today!"
>
> And, all morning, he went about looking for camels. However, at noon, he saw his shadow again, and said, "A mouse will do."
> —Kahlil Gibran

Anyone with imagination can catch the underlying meaning of these verses. Sooner or later, all of us pass through that process of personal disillusionment. Our ability is decidedly limited, and our achievements will be commonplace, at best. The fox eat a camel for lunch, probably not. A very small mouse will have to do instead.

But, there is nothing uncomplimentary about being an ordinary person. The overwhelming majority of the people about us are everyday individuals, with an ordinary mind, and ordinary personality and ordinary resources of strength and endurance. Once, intelligence tests were given to more than 1,700,000 in the Army. Of this number, a cross-section of the manhood of the nation, only 13 percent proved to have superior mental endowment. Of this gifted group, only one-third reached the highest grade on the examinations. The implication is that, of the young men in America today, only about four percent possess outstanding intellectual gifts. So let us not feel ashamed to be ordinary people. The next time an embarrassing failure convinces you that you have only an ordinary mind, remember that there is nothing unusual about that situation. Of the next 100 people you see on the street, 96 will have ordinary minds, too. Great executive ability and great success seem quite rare. The plain fact is that most people have to struggle through the day's work with the help of ordinary native gifts, and ordinary training and ordinary inspirations and incentives. When the day's work is done, they have to content themselves with an ordinary amount of appreciation, recognition and financial return. According to the Federal Income Tax returns, the great majority of people have a total income of less than $5,000 a year. So, don't be disappointed if your financial return is small…when you don't earn $10,000 a year.

The most pertinent question is, "Are ordinary people necessarily unhappy?" One of the great days in any man's life is the day when he realizes that the best things in life are within the reach of ordinary people. Here is an attitude toward life which is desperately needed today. All about us are men and women dominated by a wild and mad desire to achieve vast wealth and spectacular success. Suppose you miss the great fortune on which you have set your heart. You can still find the world filled with beauty. You can discover the splendor of simple flowers and ordinary hills, the glory of a home and the deep satisfaction that comes from working—even ordinary work—done to the best of your ability. The trouble is that so many people look at "the bluebird." The bluebird eludes. They can't find it. The significance is that the "Bluebird of Happiness" is beauty of nature, companionship of friends, love of family, joys of living.

There was a man who insisted on writing his own epitaph. It read, "Born a human being. Died a wholesale grocer." He explained, "I was so busy selling groceries that I had no time for my family and friends. I was so busy selling groceries that I had no time for the drama, for lectures, for concerts, for reading, for community service. All these areas of life were pushed out by the grocery business. I was so busy making a living, I never had time to live." This man was too busy making money. He missed many things that make life abundant. Trying to be rich outside, this man died a poor man inside. "Born a human being. Died a grocer."

Some people make the most of their ordinary abilities. They find ways of gaining extraordinary results with ordinary equipment. Though their native endowment may be only a single talent, through study and self-discipline, they learn to use that one talent so effectively that it becomes the practical equivalent of five talents. Theodore Roosevelt's career offers a striking example. To one enthusiastic admirer he wrote, "No, you are wrong about me. I am only an ordinary person, without special ability in any line. In most things I am only slightly above the average, and in many I am frankly under than over. This is certainly true of my physical equipment. I can't run. I'm only an ordinary walker and only a fair swimmer. I can probably ride a horse better than I can do anything else, but I am certainly not a remarkable horseman. Neither am I a good shot. My sight is not strong, and I have to be close to my game to get any aim at all. As far as literary gifts are concerned, I am certainly not a brilliant writer. I have written a good deal, but I always have to slave over everything I put on paper." President Roosevelt had mastered one of the fine arts of life, the art of making the most of ordinary abilities.

There are many ordinary people who do not shine as stars, but who are nevertheless making a contribution to the world. They are usually unknown but make possible the greatness of others. Marconi, the great inventor, once said that his epochal discoveries would have been impossible but for the work of a humble and unknown scientist named Tay. So, great men stand on the shoulders of little men. Somebody's achievement is rooted in another man's faithfulness. When David Livingstone was buried in London, the people were greatly impressed by a lone man standing at the head of the casket, a black man, withdrawn in his grief like a dog bereft of his master. He was the Zanzibar servant who had brought Livingstone's body from the African swamplands and accompanied it across the sea. He had helped Livingstone in many ways—in his missionary work by guiding him through jungles and protecting him in many ways. Livingstone achieved world prominence. This black man emerged out of obscurity for a single instant and then disappeared again, quickly forgotten. But the work of the one was helped forward by the faithfulness of the other.

Some time ago, there was unveiled at one of our mid-western universities, an unusual memorial tablet. It was erected in honor of a graduate who was definitely termed as "average man." During his undergraduate days, he took part in a number of university activities, but he never won a prize or an election to an important office. He tried out for football every year, but never played on the first team or took part in any of the important games. His scholastic grades averaged B, and he was not eligible for any major academic honor. But, year after year, this young man did his best. During the war, he met his death trying to rescue a wounded man under fire. Friends erected a memorial tablet at his alma mater. The inscription on that tablet is one which men of ordinary gifts would do well to ponder deeply: "HE PLAYED FOUR YEARS ON THE SCRUBS, BUT HE NEVER QUIT." He never quit. He always kept on fighting. He taught himself to make his hardest struggle when he was being beaten. Who questions that an ordinary man with that capacity is more than a match for a gifted man without it?

Yes, we are ordinary people with ordinary abilities. I am an ordinary minister. You are ordinary laymen. Our church is an ordinary church. We may not be able to do outstanding things, but we can be faithful in little things. After all, that is all expected of us. ✼

On Being Fully Alive

Waialua Pilgrim Church, 1948

Recently a young man committed suicide and he left this note: "Died of old age at 21." This young man was fed up with life at 21.

Once a 14-year-old high school girl stepped up to Dr. R. Stanley Jones after his talk and said to him, "Dr. Jones, I am like that girl you spoke about. I am inwardly empty; and worse, I am in a tangle. I have been kicked out of four schools and I am being kicked out of the present one. Is it too late to do anything now?" She asked whether it was too late to do anything at 14. Here is a girl who is messing up her life at 14.

We have but one life to live and the biggest problem in life is how to make the most of it. Voltaire once said, "Most men die without having lived." By that he meant that most men live a meaningless and worthless life and then they die. The true business of life is living. No one can dispute this fact. It is one thing to which we give every moment of every day. To know how to live is the primary objective of all knowledge.

To ask the age of another person, we would say, "How old are you?" And to answer that question, we would say, "I am 15 years old," or "I am 25 years old." Why emphasize the fact that we are getting older? Don't ask anybody, "How old are you?" That's an insult. Ask him, "How young are you?" And don't say, "I am 15 years old." Say, "I am 15 years young." After all, age is the state of mind. We ought to be getting younger each day.

The great hunger of the age in which we live is not to live longer, but to live more happily. There may be some who are absorbed in quantity of life, but most of us are interested in quality of life.

With 24 hours a day on our hands, and with but one life to live here in this world, we had better be concerned about how we can get the most out of it while it lasts. I am going to point out to you that we must do at least four things to make our life significant and meaningful.

1. In the first place, in order to make the most of life, we must have a right way of looking at it. The late Will Rogers said, "You cannot judge a man by his face. To judge a man, you must get behind him and see what he is looking at." In life, we can always find what we look for. Once a woman made a boat trip and as the boat neared the equator, she took out her spyglass. She thought that the equator was an actual line on the globe. She looked and looked but she could not see the equator. A friend of her, who was standing by, wanted to play a joke on her. She pulled a hair from her head and put it in front of the woman's spyglass and asked, "Now do you see the equator?" The woman's face beamed, "Yes, I see the equator. It is beautiful, isn't it? But I see something crawling on it!" She found what she had been looking for. There are two types of people in the world: the people who have the attitude of appreciation and the people who have the attitude of criticism. There are people who go about life criticizing things. If you say "white," they will say "black." If you say, "heart," they will say, "spade." If you say that such and such person is a fine person, they will say, "Oh, he is not so hot." They are always ready to pick on things and people to pieces. They see life as travelers see our American cities from a railroad train, at their worst, because railroads usually go through the ugliest districts of the cities. We call these people pessimists. Once I saw this letter in the *Hilo Tribune Herald*. It was written by a tourist who had visited Hilo. "Editor, *Hilo Tribune Herald:* As a newcomer, I am very much disappointed in your islands, especially in Honolulu and Hilo. Your restaurants are filthy. I was served flies, ants and hairs in them. At one hotel, I paid $1.25 per plate for a 35-cent meal in the States. Your theaters charge 40 cents for a 10-cent picture. One would at least expect fans or air-condition-

ing in a 40-cent theater. I thought I'd die for want of air the other evening. Hilo is way behind times. I have traveled extensively, but when I get back to the States next month, I will not have a word of praise for the Hawaiian Islands. I went to Coconut Island the other day and got white lice off the ground. I can prove it. Something is wrong. A mainlander." He concludes his letter by saying, "Something is wrong." The fact of the matter is that something was wrong with him. He was an incurable pessimist. What we get out of life depends on what we see in life and what we see in life depends on what we look for. God knows, we are all imperfect enough. If we go forth and find the faults of humanity, we will not be disappointed. They are all there. But why major in faults? Why not go out to discover the good in the men and women about us? We will be surprised at what a host of heroes and saints live in our homes, and shops and streets. So, if you want to get the most of life, begin tomorrow to look upon your world and your fellow men with appreciation instead of criticism. Blessed are they that look for the best, for they shall not be disappointed. Cursed are they that look for the worst, for they too shall meet their expectation.

2. In the second place, in order to get the most out of life, we must live upon all the possible areas and levels of experience. Many people remain satisfied with a bare margin of life's good things. Many people live a narrow, limited life. John Stuart Mill said that man must be happy as a man, because mere animal existence is not the permanent state of man. Man is an animal, but he is infinitely more than an animal. Once a scientist figured out that the average sized human body is worth only about 98-cents. Yes, physically, a man may be a combination of chemicals, but he is essentially a spiritual being. He is a personality. He must live happily as a man. If a man lives just to satisfy his appetites, he is no better than an animal. On one of the billboards in

the States was a picture of a big dish of steaming hot baked beans. The vapor from this appetizing portion, as it rose, formed these words, "The Joy of Living." Again, in a magazine advertisement, there was a picture of a popular brand of beer with the same words written about it, "The Joy of Living." The implication is that the joy of living consists in plenty of appetizing food and stimulating beer to eat and drink. The tragedy of the modern age is that that philosophy is being incarnated in thousands of people. They seem to live with the philosophy, "Eat, drink, and try to be merry." I say, "try," for I know they are only trying. They can never be happy. Such life is a cheese-and-crackers existence. When I was attending University of Hawai'i, I stayed in a dormitory where about 15 other college students lived. I remember that at one of the bull sessions we had a heated argument on the question of whether we live to eat or eat to live. Some maintain the thesis that we were here to eat, that eating was the main business in life. There are many things, besides eating, that we ought to enjoy as human beings. There is God's great out-of-doors, which millions live in, but never see and possess for themselves. We ought to read good books. The man who misses the joys of good literature is existing on cheese and crackers. We ought to enjoy good magazines. What kind of magazines do you read? We ought to enjoy seeing good movies. How discriminating are you in selecting the movies you see? We ought to enjoy good music. It is a pity that so many people sit by the radio for hours, listening to what comes over the radio. We ought to increase the number of our interests and the circle of our friends. We tend to go in cliques…don't care to associate with others. The man who gets the most out of life is that man who lives on all the levels of human experience: physical, spiritual, intellectual, aesthetic, emotional. Our business in life ought to be to build a well-rounded personality.

3. In the third place, you get the most out of life by putting the most into it. There are two ways to get money out of a bank. One is to hold up the bank and at the point of cold, blue steel, make your demands. Risky—and never succeeds. The other way to get money out of a bank is to put money into it. The more you put in, the more you can get out with interest. Life is like that. The more you put into it, the more you can get out. Happiness depends on giving, and not getting. Once there was a boy who was deep in friendship with a girlfriend. All of a sudden, he quit his girlfriend and when he was asked why he had quit her, he replied, "She had the 'gimmies.'" "Gimmies? What's that?" his friend asked him. "You know, gimmie this and gimmie that." Too many people have the gimmies. They are not happy because of this fact. Once there was a man who used to say this prayer every day, "Lord, bless me and my wife. My son John and his wife. Us four and no more." If we are to get the most of life, our interest in life must cease to be self-centered and find its focus in the lives of other people. When we care for others, we escape from self-centered into the love that sets us free. Modern psychology says that without this living interest in others, no personality is really developed or complete. It is a strange but true paradox of life that the more we give, the more we receive. There is a body of water in Palestine called the Dead Sea. It is called the Dead Sea because it has no outlet. It receives water from surrounding regions, but never gives out its own. Since there is no outlet, the water has become very salty. In fact, so much so that no living things can live in it. Human beings are just like that. We become dead when we get to be selfish and greedy and living only for ourselves. Dead people walking on streets. As someone said, "To live is to give."

4. Lastly, in order to get the most out of life, we must find a purpose in life so that all we do and all we strive for will be centered on that one thing. Life will lack direction and unity if we have no coordinating purpose…no goal in life. In the daily life of all of us, there is a whole series of what might be called secondary aims or objects which take possession of us from point to point. In his work, a man has one aim…which is to do his job as well as he can. At home, another aim occupies his mind…that of securing the health and well-being of his family, training of children. His leisure time may be spent in whatever kinds of recreation for body and mind that suits his particular taste. All these are secondary aims. They are right and good in their places. But, in order to make our life zestful and worthwhile, we must have some one purpose that binds them all. There is but one purpose that can do this very thing and that is God's purpose for the world. When Tolstoy Valentino was 50 years old, he felt life growing stale and meaningless. He grew despondent. He confesses that he had to hide the rope to avoid the temptation of hanging himself. One day, he was walking alone in the forest, debating with himself about God. He found that every time he thought about God, there came within him "an uprush of vital energy" and for the moment, life took on beauty and meaning. "Why do I look further," he said to himself, "He is there, He without whom one cannot live." Without God, the richest life is poor indeed.

Secrets of Married Happiness
Waialua Pilgrim Church, 1949

The very word "home" stirs the deepest sentiments in our hearts. The home is the foundation of any country/society. But, something is happening to the American home. About a century ago, divorce is almost unheard of. Today it is on the increase. It is now said that one out of every three marriages ends in divorce. It is a very high rate. Someone said, "A marriage may be holy wedlock, or an unholy deadlock, giving or getting." There are too many marriages that end in deadlocks. Someone had coined the epigram "Marry in haste and regret in leisure." But Hollywood has changed it to "Marry in haste and repeat it in leisure!" The trouble is that, to many young people, the Hollywood stars become their heroes and heroines. There in Hollywood, marriage does not seem to be thought as a sacred thing. The divine sacrament of marriage is dragged into the dust of life. We must admit that there are some instances when divorce is necessary. There are times when divorce is the only way out. But, under all circumstances, it is a sign of failure and it is a part of the sickness of our society. So, we do well to consider the secrets of married happiness.

The story of Isaac and Rebekah is a classic in the Bible. "And Isaac took Rebekah, and she became his wife and he loved her." If it were written today, it would probably read, "He loved her and she became his wife." Our stories and plays and movies condition our thinking. The hero and the heroine, after overcoming many obstacles usually a villain or villains, get married. Romance comes to its climax in marriage. After the climax, we lose interest in the story. We take it for granted that they "live happily ever after." But, in actual life, that does not always happen. It has rough places. Married life is not all roses and romances.

Marriage will not fail nor the home break apart, as long as we can say, "And she became his wife, and he loved her."

After all, love is the foundation of successful home and family life. There are some who say that life can be described in three words, "Yells, bells and knells"…births, marriages and deaths. Yes, from one viewpoint, that is it. But, how much more there is if we can add, "She loved him."

I would like to say three things we do well to keep in mind in order to be happy in marriage.

First of all, we must understand and realize that marriage is a partnership. It is sharing of life together. Once a man said in public, "I am the head of my family." His friends, who heard him say that, thought he was dominating his wife. One of them told his wife that her husband had said that he was the head of the family. She said, "Well, my husband may be the head of our family, but I am the neck. I tell the head which direction to go." When one party dominates the other, there is bound to be friction and discord. Once a young bride sent a telegram on her honeymoon to her mother, it read: "Arrived here safe and sound. Had a grand row before dinner." And her mother wailed, "Think of it, they're quarreling already." Of course, she forgot that the suspected word might stand also for a boat "row" where two people have to pull together if they are to arrive at their destination.

A famous authority on marriage made a study of 2600 marriages that has stood the test of five years (the first five years, figures indicate, are the hardest). One thing he wanted to know was who dominated in the home. He said, "The figures leave no doubt that a democratic co-partnership is associated with the greatest happiness." Where there is cooperation, or where there is democracy, there is bound to be happiness.

The husband and wife ought to have some interests that they can share together. They ought to do many things together. The author of an article in a magazine article, "How To Be a Swell Wife," says, "What kind of husband have you? Figure him out. If he is a gadabout, join him and be a gadabout yourself. If he is a stay-at-home, you can learn to stay at home, too, and find it very pleasant…. In golf, your approach shots are important. Well, so are they in marriage. How about the way you approach your husband? Watch his moods and play to them. Cultivate a soothing voice that goes straight to his heart. Never ask for anything when your husband is tired from a hard day at the office. Wait until he is at peace with the world and your arms are around him, before bringing up the subject of a new dress, a diamond ring, or trip to Coney Island…. Does your husband like to play golf or tennis, or fish or swim or go in for any game? If so, provided your health will permit, learn to play the same games…not only to be able to play with him (for he won't always want you) but just so you will be able to discuss the game with him intelligently. He wants a pal…be one." Of course, this is for the wife. The husband, in turn, should take interest in what his wife is doing. If the wife is interested in cooking, he should take some interest in cooking, at least enough interest in it to want to help do the dishes. To confess, I do not always do this. Everything has to be worked out together. The money matter is one of the important matters in marriage. The financial ways of a family help or hinder the success of the family. There must be teamwork.

Bridegroom: "And now, dear, that we are married, let us have a clear understanding about our affairs. Do you wish to be president or vice-president?

Bride: "Neither. You will be both. I'll just be the treasurer."

The inability to handle their finances has broken many a home. The wife should never beg for money. The husband should not hand the paycheck to his wife and let her dole to him his pocket money. A consultant asked a disturbed couple how they spent their money. The husband said, "Well, 30 percent for rent, 30 percent for food, 30 percent for clothing, and 30 percent for pleasure." When the consultant pointed out the 120 percent total, the man said, "That's where our trouble is." They should work out a budget and stay within the budget.

In a word, to be happy, a marriage must be a partnership, an honest sharing of life, its experiences and expenses, its responsibilities and renunciations, its joys and sorrows. When one party desires to dominate, it ceases to be a duet and becomes a solo, or rather a discord.

Secondly, to succeed in marriage, the husband and wife must be the right kind of person. It is not the marriage which fails. It is the people who undertake it who fail in this intimate relationship of life. The most important secret of married happiness lies in the character of the people who make up a home. The trouble is not with marriage, but with the people who embrace it.

Someone said, "Life is an 'inside job.' If we cannot live with ourselves and keep the peace, we cannot live with anyone else without friction." In marital relations, as in all other relations, we need personal qualities, such as considerateness, patience, unselfishness, forgiveness, etc.

A Harvard professor says that he would "be prepared to reduce by 50 percent the divorces in the modern world if he could have young couples entering marriage know in advance that 'differences were bound to spring up' and that they are 'a sign of love's health, not its mortal ill.'" Difficulties and differences are bound to come up. Marriage involves tension or conflict, adjustments between two lives, which are seeing to be one. The thing to remember is that two people who live with each other do not always have to agree. As someone puts it, "We agree to differ, but we insist upon our right to love one another just the same." When differences come up, there should be no nagging, scolding and sullen carrying of grudges. There should be patience, considerateness of the other person and forgiveness. "Never yell at each other unless the house is on fire."

There is room for honest disagreement between two people. There was a time when a wife was supposed to agree with her husband on almost everything. But the time has changed. Perhaps some men may be saying, "Backward, turn backward, to time, in thy flight." A man said recently, "I always have the last word in our family and it is this, 'You're right!'" One of the hardest things in the married life is to admit that we are wrong and someone else is right. We can save endless heartache and trouble if we admit that we are wrong.

Abraham Lincoln had a very unhappy home life. He had a wife who complained, criticized and nagged about everything that Lincoln did. He was stoop-shouldered; he walked awkwardly and lifted his feet straight up and down. There was no grace in his movement. She didn't like the way his huge ears stood out at right angles from his head. His nose wasn't straight, his lower lip stick out. He looked consumptive and his feet and hands were too large, his head too small. But, his forgiveness and big-heartedness saved his home. Once he told his friend of the argument he just had with his wife about the color they should paint their house. His wife insisted that they should paint it yellow. He wanted it painted green. "What did you do?" asked his friend. "We compromised," said Lincoln. "And what color did you paint it?" asked his friend. Lincoln answered, "We painted it yellow."

Married happiness requires that each forget himself for the other. Once a young girl wrote to a newspaper and asked, "What must I do to win and hold a man?" The newspaper replied, "Learn 400 ways of saying, 'I think you are wonderful!'" The psychology of that answer is correct. She was to learn to forget herself for the sake of the other. No marriage can succeed unless the two people exercise patience, considerateness, forgiveness, unselfishness. In a word, they must be right kind of persons.

Thirdly, to succeed in marriage, we need the stabilizing power of religion. If we are to make a happy home, we must start with God. I am convinced that no marriage can ever last until it was brought into it a religious influence. Religion gives stability to one's home. Where there is religion, there is unity and strength. Religion spiritualizes married life and lifts it on a high place. Susannah Wesley had 17 children, but she found time to sit down alone with each one of them to tell him about great things of God. The result was that out of her family came Charles and John Wesley, both world famous men. Religion elevates all that happens in the homes, gives it an atmosphere of tolerance and friendliness. Happy are the man and woman who can come to church worship service together. When they worship God together, somehow help comes from above and an unseen power binds them together. Happy are the man and woman who are spiritually bound in God.

LIVIING PEACEABLY WITH OTHERS
'Ewa Community Church, 1951

If possible, so far as it depends upon you, live peaceably with all. The hardest thing in the world for all of us is to live in right relationships with each other, without jealousy, friction or misunderstanding. The biggest problem in life is how to get along with other people. We all acknowledge the difficulty of getting along with other people. The causes of human conflict and tension are many and infinitely complex and deeply rooted in men. Every day, our wills collide with other wills. Every day our powerful drives for recognition, for security, for power and dominance are contested and thwarted by someone.
Every day we meet people who do not think the way we do. Every day we meet people with whom we disagree on some subjects. Yes, being at peace with all men is the hardest thing in the world. At times we find it hard to get along with certain people because of the hatreds and prejudices we inherit. At other times, the trouble between people is caused by wounded pride, by jealousy, fatigue, sickness and overwrought nerves. Sometimes we dislike people the instant we meet them. Perhaps it is because each personality gives off subtle radiations which attract or repel.

There is no simple solution to this problem of getting along with others. The ability to get along peaceably with others is not something we are born with. It is something we learn. It is a skill acquired the hard way…by practice, application and effort and by self-discipline. It is a precarious achievement of the human spirit. Shakespeare once said, "Heat not a furnace for your foe so hot that it singes yourself." We often give way to unkind impulse when we are cross or injured. We become furious when we are hurt and immediately we try to get even. We become bilious and unhappy when we entertain a grudge. When we have an intense prejudice, we become filled with hatred. But we do well to remember that what the other fellow does to us is never damaging as what we do to ourselves. The deadliest of wounds are self-inflicted. We are the losers. We injure ourselves emotionally, spiritually with poison. Four men who engaged in the discovery of anesthesia, came to grief because of their quarrels and jealousies. Wells committed suicide in prison. Long died suddenly in embitterment. Jackson's hatred of Morton is said to have brought him to a lunatic asylum. And Morton died of a stroke induced by reading one of Jackson's attacks on him. Each of the four men was stricken and cut down by the poison of his vindictive spirit. "Heat not a furnace for your foe so hot that it singes yourself."

    Abraham Lincoln once said, "No man resolved to make the most of himself can spare the time for personal contention. Still less can he afford to take all the consequences, including the vitiating of his temper and the loss of self-control." We cannot help stepping on each other's toes. We cannot help meeting head-on in dispute and controversy. We cannot help being rubbed the wrong way occasionally by people. We cannot help having our purposes thwarted and our plans spoiled. We are individuals and no two persons are exactly alike, physically, mentally or emotionally. No two persons think exactly alike. We are bound to have disagreements. Once a man said, "My wife and I have been married for 30 years and we have never had any disagreement." What a boring and monotonous life he and his wife must have been living.

    When we hate our enemies, we actually hurt ourselves. We do not sleep well. We lose our appetites. Our blood pressure goes up. Our health is impaired. Our days and nights are turned into turmoil. Even our looks become hardened. When Jesus said, "Love your enemies," he was giving us, not only high ethics, but sound medical advice. A freshman took his father to a college football game. "Father," he said as they took their seats, "You'll see more excitement for your two dollars than you ever saw before." "Oh, I don't know," grunted the parent, "Two dollars was all I paid for my marriage license."

    The point is how we are to behave when we have conflicts with others. One day a workman in a laboratory dropped a beautiful silver cup into a jar of strong acid, where it gradually dissolved and disappeared. But, the chemist put a chemical mixture into the jar, and in a little while, every particle of silver settled on the bottom. Then, he drained off the acid, sent the precious metal to a silversmith, and soon the cup was restored to its original form.

This incident is a parable. If a man has the right spirit, he can get along with other people in any situation. He doesn't have to play dirty. He doesn't have to fly off the handle. He doesn't have to become cantankerous. He doesn't have to let ill will and hatred tear him to pieces. He can control himself. He doesn't have to hit back. He can do what Lincoln did, who used the fight he had in him, not to get even, but to solve the problem. Or, he can repay the injury with kindness. Nobody has to be hard because life is hard. Rossini the great musician said, "Give me a laundry list and I will set it to music."

I am sure something like this was in the mind of Jesus when he said in the Beatitudes, "Blessed are the peacemakers for they shall be called the children of God." He was thinking of men who, instead of returning evil for evil, return evil with good. He was not thinking of men who, with placid amiability, shut their eyes to the evils of society, who are so careful not to irritate anybody that he agreed with others on every subject.

No society can ever be secured that does not have a strong minority of disciplined, unselfish, charitable people. "Blessed are the peacemakers for they shall be called the children of God." This beatitude, like all the rest, is basic as a principle of social hygiene. Walter Lippman was right when he said that we have no national problems which are inherently insoluble. We could settle most of them if it were possible to break through the barriers of intolerance and self-interest. The trouble is that we don't have the capacity to differ without denunciation, the capacity to argue without impugning motives.

The quickest formula for losing everything is to hold on to the good things we enjoy and not to share them with others. No nation, or group within a nation, can maintain its privileges except by sharing them. Without mass purchasing power, factories shut down. Unless we are willing to buy the goods and services of other people, they cannot buy ours. If large sections of the population are denied their rights to life, liberty and the pursuit of happiness, it is bad for them, of course, and ultimately bad for all of us. Freedom, prosperity and peace are shared by all—or forfeited by all. Without altruism, a society will collapse. This principle holds true in international affairs. The problem of world peace is a vital problem today. Millions of people all over the world are living in dread of another world war. If you want to spend some leisure hours to good purpose, read the history of the United States in the latter part of the 18th century. It is an exciting story how, after throwing off the British yoke, the colonies fell to quarreling among themselves; how commerce was crippled by tariff barriers and currency differentials; how the whole financial structures of the country went to pieces and there was no authority to set up a sound and uniform fiscal policy or put down civil strife; and how finally, in desperation, the states delegated their most important sovereign power to the central government, and order was restored. The issue they faced in 1787 we face now. But, in our day, it is international in scope. With 60-odd nations claiming sovereign rights in a shrinking world, the upshot is not peace, but conflict and anarchy. Right now we are pinning our hope on the United Nations. We need such an organization as the U.N. to deal with problems of international concern, such as disputes between countries, tariffs, armaments, the administration of colonial territory and strategic areas. There is not a cheap way to establish world peace. It calls for greater sacrifice on the part of nations than is required to win a war. Nations, both big and small, must be willing to submit themselves to a system of justice administered by the impartial authority of the U.N.

    Pierre van Paseen has a story of two missionaries in Borneo. One was German, the other French. They lived in perfect harmony until finally the traders brought them news of the first world war. Then they became estranged, suspicious of each other, and actually harbored thoughts of killing. One afternoon, several weeks later, they both arrived at the chapel at the same time to ring the bell for vespers. As they reached for the rope, their hands touched. For a brief moment, there was a deadly silence—then they embraced. They became friends once more.

The early colonists considered the Indians only as savages to be exterminated as quickly as possible. But, the Quakers looked upon them as children of God and treated them as such. The book *Yang and Yin* tells of an American doctor in a Chinese mission hospital. A tubercular patient was stricken suddenly with appendicitis. The hospital was not equipped with a pulmotor. And the American doctor, fully aware of the risk, stooped down and forced his own breath into the patient's lungs—and the man was saved. The doctor's Chinese assistant, was horrified at this carelessness on the American doctor's part. It was Christian love—the recognition of the worth of man. A man can do this without quarrel or conflict. Nobody has to be belligerent or touchy or bilious just because he finds himself in conflict with others. He does not have to be vindictive. He ought to exercise this spirit of goodwill.

Are You Impatient?

'Ewa Community Church, 1954

A professor once asked 3,000 people, "What have you to live for?" He was shocked to find that 94 percent of them were simply enduring the present while they lived for the future. Some said they were waiting for "something to happen." Others said they were waiting for their children to grow up and leave home. Still others said they were waiting for someone to die. Many were waiting for the time to take a long-dreamed-of trip. Some were simply waiting for next year to roll around.

There are many reasons why there are so many people who simply endure the present while they wait for the future. Many of them don't realize that all anyone ever has is today. They don't realize that they should live for the present as well as for the future. Of course, there are those who are forced by the events of life to stand and wait. There are those who wait as they seek for bigger things. And the problem of patience becomes real. We must learn to be patient. It is important that we do not confuse patience with laziness or indifference. It means rather, an attitude toward people and things that can be creative and enriching.

Let us consider several aspects of mastering the art of patience.

1. In the first place, let us remember that we can always endure more than we think we can. A distinguished engineer and scientist tell of an experience in one of the laboratories under his direction. He had been looking for stronger steels and had been testing a good many samples. One day he gave a new sample to one of his men. He told the assistant to drill it to get some shavings for metallurgical tests. A few days later he asked the assistant if he had drilled the piece of steel. "No," the assistant said, "It is too hard. You can't drill that." Then he asked him, "Did you try a diamond-pointed

drill?" No, he hadn't tried that. So, they tried it and got some shavings for the tests. He said, "The steel wasn't too hard; the drill was too soft." This is so often true with us. The experiences we complain about are not too hard. We are too soft. Then we come up against some harsh, untried experience of life, we think we can't make it. We need to know that God had given us diamond-pointed tools of faith that can cut their way through any situation. There is power like that in patience. This applies not only to the disasters of life. It applies especially to our ambitions and hopes for ourselves and for our world. God gives us always the capacity to stand more than we think we can.

Michelangelo, who was lame and had a broken nose, for 20 months lay flat on his back on a scaffolding in the Sistine Chapel painting the murals. He stopped to eat and sleep only when he was about to fall from the platform with exhaustion. He threw himself into bed with his clothes on, not taking off his shoes for weeks. When he did, the skin peeled off with them. In 20 months, without assistance, he completed all the 343 figures on the ceiling; a task so vast that its completion is still beyond belief. It is always so. The trouble is, many of us do not have the endurance to be patient. When life challenges us to be patient, it does not ask us to take it easy. Patience sometimes demands sacrifice. It exacts a heavy price. But, it must be paid. We must be willing to pay the price.

2. In the second place, let us remember that we can always find hidden values in any situation. We all suffer under the delusion that we will be happy when we arrive at a certain destination, when our schooling is completed, when we get a better job, when we are married, when we recover from illness, when we buy a home, when some disagreeable job is finished or when all our bills are paid.

Then we discover, to our surprise, that life has a way of facing us with new complications as fast as old ones are settled. We need to learn that even these periods of waiting may be fruitful themselves. We must find happiness where we are, or we are likely to miss it altogether. We can use our times of patience. They have much to teach us if we have the grace to learn. They can mean much to our own well-being and growth. A man was put to bed with a serious sickness (tuberculosis) for two years at the peak of his powers. He was patient. He became well again. He said, "A good case of sickness is better than a college education!" Some time ago, I was sick in bed for about a year. I was forced to be flat on my back for one year. As I look back, I can say that it was one of the most fruitful years of my life. I learned the meaning of suffering. I had time to think, meditate and pray. I had time to read books.

Some years ago a young man was very dissatisfied with his job. He was an artist. But, the routine of his everyday tasks as a magazine illustrator bored him to death. However, in his spare time, he began to experiment on his own. He drew pictures on cards. One day, he showed the idea to an editor for whom he was working. He took a pack of his cards. On each card was the picture of a rabbit, nothing more. Then he flipped the cards rapidly. The rabbit seemed to jump and run away. The editor made fun of the idea. He should not have done so, however, for it was Walt Disney with the beginnings of his moving picture animations. He was using his waiting period by working on his idea at night in his garage.

There are always hidden values in any situation. No period of patience need be unproductive. We should find life good anytime.

3. In the third place, let us remember that we can always afford to wait for larger goals if we have faith in God. Once a small boy was watching a telephone repairman on a pole. The man was connecting a test set and trying the connection with the test board up at the exchange office. After listening a few minutes, the boy rushed back into the house screaming, "Mama, come out here quick! There's a man on a telephone pole talking to heaven." "What makes you think he's talking to heaven?" asked the mother. He answered, "Because he hollered, 'Hello! Hello! Hello! Good Lord! What's the matter up there? Can't anyone hear?'" It sounds just like a lot of impatient people barking at heaven to hurry up and do something about everything. Many of us have big plans and we want to get on with them. We don't like to wait. We want to be going somewhere and doing something. We become irksome when someone tells us to be patient. We insist on running even if we do nothing but run around in circles. There are times when we get farther by standing still. Once a famous artist-philosopher announced the opening of a lecture course. A large group of students gathered at the studio at the appointed hour. The door was locked, and on it was a sign saying that the meeting had been postponed. On the second appointed date, only about half the original number of students showed up. Again, the door was locked, and again there was a notice of postponement. On the third appointed date, only a small number of students came at all. Ruskin told them that the postponements were for the purpose of discouraging those who did not have the patience to show a real desire for the work. He said, "I think the class is now sufficiently winnowed down. Let us go to work."

Life is like that. Sometimes, the choicest rewards are withheld because we have not been willing to wait. We all stand before closed doors. Too often, we turn away before they open.

4. In the last place, let us remember that we can always trust and serve God, wherever we are and whatever we do. When Central Union Church erected the new building, which now stands on the corner of Beretania Street and Punahou Street, the architect asked the pastor to select an inscription for the chancel high above the central cross. In order to fit the space, it had to be exactly 18 letters and spaces in length. After considerable search and research, the pastor chose words that he felt would fit any and every person and situation. The words chosen were, "LOVE NEVER FAILETH." Eighteen letters and spaces. These words have a special meaning, perhaps, for all who are called upon to walk the ways of patience. No matter how confused or uncertain the way, the love of God is ours to sustain and guide us. God's love never fails. As we learn to trust Him, our impatience dies away. A doctor tells of an elderly woman who was knocked down by a tire, which flew off a passing truck. Her hip was broken, certainly through no fault of her own. Her active days were at an end. When the doctor went to see her in the hospital, she looked up out of great pain and said with a wonderful smile, "Well, I wonder what God has for me to do here." She began to spread the cheer of a shining faith in the hospital ward. She began to give her words of comfort to the other patients in her ward.

Yes, love never fails those who are patient enough to know the presence of God under all circumstances. There are times when our work, our ideals, our faith seem to pull on us. We wonder if there is any use in keeping on. We are tempted to get out from under our responsibilities and give up the whole thing. Sometimes our setbacks are heartbreaking. Our limitations are many. But, we need to know that the battles of society are won by patient, plodding effort. It is the day-by-day, ceaseless, never-ending labor that guarantees victory. Few of us get a chance to do spectacular things but all of us can live honestly, quietly, faithfully, day by day. And, if we keep at it, if we do not give up, if we patiently endure to the end, God will reward us with a victory of faith and love.

How Are Your Nerves?
'Ewa Community Church, 1954

Nerves are one thing we all have in common. The only difference is that some people are more conscious of their nerves than others. And some of us are more conscious of our nerves at one time than another. The world we live in is not a natural friend of our nerves. In fact, it is the avowed enemy of our nerves. We talk too much. We talk too loudly. We run the radio too continuously. We run the TV too long. We move too fast. We are always busy, doing things and going places. We have too many "new-fangled" noises that are unfriendly to our nerves. We have the comforts and gadgets of civilization but they have not brought us true happiness and peace. We have machines that help us save time, but we don't know what to do with the time we have saved. We are so restless. And even the pleasures we seek leave us jittery and unsatisfied. I believe more people are highly strung and nervously irritable than ever before. Modern life is characterized by lack of serenity. It is not easy to achieve inner peace today. We are geared to high-tension living. Nowadays the people are so keyed up and nervous that they don't even sleep in church when a dull sermon is being preached.

Talking about sleeping in the church reminds me of a story. Once a man went to his physician for advice as to how he could be cured of the bad habit of snoring. The doctor asked him, "Does your snoring disturb your wife?" "Does it disturb my wife?" echoed the man, "Why, it disturbs the whole congregation."

The production of sleeping pills has multiplied four times in the past 20 years. Each year 350 tons of sleeping pills are made in the United States. It is enough to put everyone in the country to sleep for 22 nights a year, enough to put nine million people to sleep 365 nights a year. Isn't this indicative of the fact that the people are getting keyed up and nervous? Does this show that life is getting so unhappy that normal people must take drugs to put them to sleep? Once a man seated himself in the dentist's chair and exclaimed, "Thank God for the opportunity once in a while to drop into the dentist's chair and relax."

There was a doctor who had a nervous breakdown. His doctors said he was doing too much and that he must give up much of his work. He was flat on his back, but he said he heard God speaking to him even as He had spoken to Moses, "My presence will go with thee, and I will give you rest." He believed that and went back to work. He took as the motto of his life, "Let go and let God in." Today he is doing even more than ever before and is in perfect health.

If there is one lesson this generation needs to learn, it is how to take time to live. Even though the world we live in is not friendly to our nerves, the cure for a troubled mind is not to be found so much in changing our environment as in changing ourselves. Steady nerves and a quiet mind are not things we go out and find. They are things we create. That is why in the same noisy world we see people who are upset most of the time, and we see other people who are cool, calm, collected and inwardly quiet. Abraham Lincoln and Edwin Stanton lived in the same world under the same pressures, stresses and strains. Yet, whatever happened outwardly, Lincoln remained quiet inwardly, whereas Stanton, if he was not upset all the time, was ready to be upset at a moment's notice.

A popular magazine stated recently, "Businessmen who are constantly tired may be on the verge of a breakdown." An examination of over 2,000 tired businessmen by Philadelphia's Franklin Clinic found many suffering from hypertension. Cure = Relaxation. But, the trouble is that they don't know how to relax. A former governor and wartime ambassador to Great Britain took his life and an editorial writer said of him, "He was a tired man. He went back to rest, but unhappily, he had forgotten how to rest." The tragedy of modern life is that many of us have forgotten to rest and relax. A psychologist says that one way to quiet our nerves is to learn to collapse physically. He says, "Let go every muscle in the body. Form a mental picture of a huge burlap bag of potatoes. Then mentally cut the bag, allowing the potatoes to roll out. What is more relaxed than an empty burlap bag?"

Often our edgy nerves are due to the fact that we have a wrong attitude toward life. We don't see ourselves in the right place. We get mixed up in the relative values of things. We see one thing to the total exclusion of everything else. We don't see anything in its right relationship. We think we are right, and we are deadly impatient with anyone who disagrees or thinks that we are wrong. We often carry a grudge or resentment. We often carry a chip on our shoulders. We feel that the world is against us. We are often beset with jealousy, which keeps our nerves on edge. We become upset the moment we see someone having something we want or someone doing something and assuming responsibilities which we are too lazy to assume.

Once a physician said, "Many of my patients have nothing wrong with them except their thoughts. So, I have a favorite prescription that I write for some. But it is not a prescription that you can fill at a drugstore. The prescription I write is a verse from the Bible, Romans 12:2. I do not write out that verse for my patients. I make them look it up and read it… 'Be ye transformed by the renewing of your mind.' To be happier and healthier they need a renewing of their minds. When they 'take' this prescription, they actually achieve a mind full of peace. That helps to produce health and well-being." A right attitude and right thinking.

In order to be quiet inwardly and to have stable nerves, we must do another thing. We must take time to be alone. Most of us are not alone often enough. We are in a crowd all day, and some of us all evening. There is an executive of a large corporation who is a very busy man, who takes some time every day to leave his office, his ringing telephone and his constant interruptions, to go up to a little room on the roof, high above the noise of the factory, where he can look out over the city to the mountains beyond. Above the noise going on below, he becomes inwardly quiet, calm and composed, so that when he descends to the noise below, an hour or so later, he exhibits a commanding poise and an undisturbable peace.

There are plenty of places we can put ourselves even for a few moments which will develop an inner self-control. Emerson said, "It is very seldom that a man is truly alone. There is one means of procuring solitude which, to me, and I apprehend it to all men, is effectual, and that is to go to the window and look at the stars." To sit in a church even when it is full of people, and sit quietly, is enough to quiet you down. A great psychologist recommended frequent attendance of chapel to his philosophy students. He told the students that the practice of going to a quiet place, which was suggestive of contemplative thought, aided in keeping one's point of view right side up. Nowadays, not only psychologists, but physicians, are recommending church attendance to their patients. It has a great value in making us quiet within and also in helping us to get a right perspective in life.

Dr. Norman Vincent Peale tells about a salesman who told him that on a business trip, he had gone to his hotel room, terribly nervous. "I tried to write some letters, but couldn't get my mind on them. I paced the room, tried to read the paper, finally decided to go down for a drink—anything to get away from myself. Then I noticed the Bible on the dresser. I hadn't read one in years, but something impelled me. I opened the book to a psalm. I read it standing up, and then sat down to read another. Soon I came to the 23rd Psalm. I had learned it as a boy in Sunday school and was surprised that I knew most of it by heart. I said it over, 'He leadeth me beside the still waters. He restoreth my soul…' I sat there repeating the words—and next thing I knew, I woke up. Apparently I had dropped off to sleep. Only about 15 minutes had passed but I was as refreshed as if I had had a good night's sleep. Then I realized for the first time in a long while, I felt at peace." One sure secret of gaining inner serenity and strength is to turn our thoughts to God. It is still true that God is the best cure for a troubled mind.

No Man is an Island

'Ewa Community Church, 1958

One great thing most desired in life is that state or quality of life we call happiness. Upon the arrival of the New Year we wish each other happiness by saying, "Happy New Year!" Happiness is the root motive underlying all our labor and struggle. People dream of happiness. They plan for it. They spend their lives in a never-ending search for it. We are all seeking happiness whether we are conscious of it or not. But the trouble is that happiness is an elusive thing. We all see happiness. We all look for it. But a very few find it.

The biggest obstacle to the attainment of happiness is one little letter in the alphabet called, "I." This happened in a classroom. The teacher was showing the class that the inventions such as airplanes, movies, radio and television were recent, which a few years ago did not exist. She asked, "What is in the world now which was not here 50 years ago?" Quick as a flash the hand of John went up. His answer was "Me." There is a young philosopher for you. He knows what the most important of all new things that have ever come to earth—me.

The other members of the family of this letter "I" are "me," "my" and "mine." This letter the dictionary describes as the personal pronoun, first singular, nominative case "by which a speaker or writer denotes himself." We are plagued by the tendency to overuse this pronoun. According to statistics, this first personal pronoun "I" is more frequently used in the telephone conversations than any other word. Once there was a man who talked to himself all the time and when he was asked why he talked to himself so much, he answered and said, "For two reasons: First, I like to talk to a smart man; second, I like to hear a smart man talk." Yes, we all love ourselves, don't we?

Some time ago, I read in our *'Ewa Hurricane*, the bi-weekly paper of the 'Ewa Plantation, a little article entitled, "Isn't It Funny?" Perhaps some of you have read it. When the other fellow takes a long time to do something, he's slow. But when I take a long time to do something, I'm thorough. When the other fellow doesn't do it, he's too lazy. But when I don't do it, I'm too busy. When the other fellow goes ahead and does something without being told, he's overstepping his bounds. But when I go ahead and do something without being told, that's initiative. When the other fellow overlooks a few of the rules of etiquette, he's rude. But when I skip a few of the rules, I'm original. When the other fellow does something that pleases the boss, he's polishing the brass. But when I do something that pleases the boss, that's cooperation. When the other fellow gets ahead, he sure had the lucky breaks. But when I manage to get ahead, Man! Hard work did it! FUNNY, ISN'T IT? OR IS IT? (Unknown Author) Well, we all rate ourselves very high, don't we? We all have a high estimate of ourselves.

No man is an island. We must grant that man is egocentric. Alongside this deep-seated selfishness there is something else—the need of comradeship. Once, a little boy was playing in the backyard. He was all alone. He had no sisters or brothers. He said to his mother, "Mother, I wish I were two puppies, so that I could play together." That child's remark is psychologically sound. We crave comradeship and companionship. We are made that way. We are social beings. We need others for our own growth and fulfillment. I am sure you have heard about a couple with no children, who prayed every day, "Lord, bless us two, and that will do." A couple of blocks farther down the street lived an old bachelor and he prayed, "Lord, bless only me, that's as far as I can see." Many people are unhappy and miserable, because they are self-centered. Their concern is only for themselves.

No man is an island. He lives in society with other people. He lives in relationships with others. Abraham Lincoln once said, "All that I am and hope to be I owe to my angel mother." We can say the same thing of ourselves. All that we are and hope to be we owe to our parents, brother, sisters, friends, teachers and benefactors. Our environment, all that surround us, our family our friends, school church and community exert a tremendous influence upon us.

To be happy, we must be in good relationships with others. In our home we cannot keep on saying, "I," "me," "my" and "mine." We must learn to say, "we," "our" and "ours." We must learn to cooperate with others and other members of our family. In our school, church and in our community we must learn to cooperate with others, work together with others. To be happy we must seek to promote the welfare of other people.

There was an elderly woman who was told by her physician that because of her heart condition she had only one year to live. She had worked hard and had saved money. When she learned of her fate, she set aside $10,000 to spend on herself, in that last year in search of happiness. People told her to travel, but she didn't like to travel. People told her to buy new clothes, but clothes did not interest her. They told her to buy a new home and a car, but she said the ones she had were in good condition. They told her to go in for nightlife, but she said that whenever she gambled, she always won. She couldn't spend money that way. She had set aside money to spend so that she could be happy for one year before her death, but didn't know how to spend the money. She is typical of millions of people in the world. She had money to live on. But she lacked the one condition of a happy life. She had no concern for others. To be happy we must identify ourselves with other people.

Dr. Harry Emerson Fosdick in his book, *On Being A Real Person*, says, "A person who has genuinely identified himself with other persons has done something of first-rate importance for himself." He goes on to say that a man who is selfish and self-centered is like a man living in a room surrounded by mirrors. Everywhere he turns, he sees himself. He is miserable because he sees nothing but himself.

A drama critic said, "No one, I am convinced, can be happy who lives only for himself. The joy of living comes from immersion in something that we know to be bigger, better, more enduring and worthier than we are.... The only true happiness comes from squandering ourselves for others." Now that's not in the Bible, but it speaks the authentic word of God about the conditions of happiness. The tragedy of life is that this simple idea is frequently forgotten and overlooked. As the result millions of people seek happiness where they can never find it. They try awfully hard to be happy. They try hard to be happy by having a good time, eating, drinking and making merry. Then there are those who struggle desperately to pile up enough money, thinking that in money is their happiness. To be sure, money can do a lot of good. Right now I am trying to collect $150 to help a promising young man in a Christian church in Japan to go into Christian ministry. This young man wants very much to go to a seminary to become a minister but he has no money. He needs $150 for his board and tuition for a year. His father died when he was a child. His mother is making dolls and things at home to help support the family. Yes, money used rightly will do a lot of good; it can contribute to our happiness and happiness of others. But if our happiness is dependent exclusively on money and the things that money can buy, it is based on insecure foundations.

 A professor once questioned a group of some 500 college students as to their aim in life. One student said, "To get ahead." Another student said, "To go places." Still another said, "To make good." It is a discouraging comment, not only on college students, but on all mankind that of all these choices young men could offer as their aim in life was some hazy ambition to advance themselves beyond their fellow men. Sometime ago I read an article in a magazine. In the article, there were three examples of people previously unhappy who, because they let the law of unselfishness work in their lives, found a way to meaningful and happy living. The first was an elderly woman who had spent years placing flowers every week on her son's grave. At the suggestion of the cemetery clerk she discovered a new reason for living by sharing the beauty of the flowers with living people. The second was a hapless, unattractive college girl who found new happiness by acquiring an interest in and concern for other people. The third was a man, a habitual drunkard, who won a victory over the curse of drink by helping another get rid of its clutches. All of these found newness of life because they redirected their lives outward, away from themselves, into the lives of others. ✺

Things That Money Cannot Buy

Nuʻuanu Congregational Church, 1960

I suppose many of you went to the carnival. We went to a carnival last night. Went to the main show first then walked around the place where they had booths of all kinds. Our youngster rode on the kiddie cars and pony. Then one of them tried the baseball throw. We also visited other booths. We had a great time. Everything cost money. I don't know how much we spent at the carnival. Yes, it is good to have money and the things that money can buy. But it is good once in a while to check to be sure that we have not lost the things that money cannot buy.

Money can buy a lot of things: food, house, school, clothes, music lessons, travel (went to Europe in 1939, visited many countries learned a lot, but cost about $2,000 and came home broke), money to help others. Money to run a church. Money can buy a lot of things we really need.

But we do well to check up once in a while to be sure we have not lost the things that many cannot buy. We live in a money-minded world. "Take out a half dollar." On this coin are the words, "In God We Trust." Many do not trust God. Trust God. Not GOD, but GOLD. Almost everything in life is conceived in terms of money. Major problems of life are conceived in terms of money. We read about burglaries and robberies in Honolulu. Wartime, people had no money. Now some people don't have money, they break into other people's houses to steal money. Crimes are committed because of money. People go insane because of worries about money. War—fundamental cause is economic, nations do not go to war because of ideologies, ideals, raw materials—they try to get what they don't have and other countries have. It is foolish to minimize the importance of money. It is foolish to underrate the importance of money. We live in a money-minded world. People are obsessed with the economic aspect of life. We don't have to tell people about the importance of money. We don't have to emphasize the importance of economic aspect of life. They all know it—know it too well.

But we do need to emphasize the other side of the matter. It is often forgotten or crowded out. We tend to forget that the things that money cannot buy are more important than the things that money can buy. "Man's life does not consist in the abundance of the things he possesses." "Man should not live by bread alone, but by every word that proceedeth out of the mouth of God." We can't live by material things of life—we are spiritual beings—different from other animals.

It is good to have money and the things that money can buy, but it is good to check up once in a while to see that we have not lost the things that money can't buy.

Now what are some of the things that money can't buy? There are many things—but I shall mention four important things.

1. Money cannot buy character. "A good name is rather to be had than great riches." It is one thing that money cannot buy. It is above price. We do well to guard our name. Must not do anything to bring a black mark on our good name. Shakespeare said, "The purest treasure mortals can afford, is spotless reputation; men are but gilded loan, or painted clay." Character that accompanies a good name is the crown and glory of life. It is the noblest possession. One of the worst dangers connected with our present obsession with the economic aspect of life is the idea that money makes a man. When we see a man living in a nice house, we think a great deal of him, we admire him. When we see a man driving around in a nice car, we admire him, a big shot. If we don't have money we tend to think that we are a failure. If we have a lot of money we think that we are a great success. Of course, admit that poverty does profoundly affect character. Children brought up in the slums have a terrible handicap. The apothecary in *Romeo and Juliet*, where, as against the law, he sells the dangerous drug, and says, "My poverty, but not my will, consents." But

on the other hand, there are many men and women coming from poverty, achieved great character. Lincoln. Character does not depend on things that money can buy. We can be without money, without things and still be a real person. Helen Keller was without sight, hearing, speech, yet was a great person. Dr. Trudeau was without health—tuberculosis in a sanitarium, one of the benefactors of humanity. Kavanagh—without arms and legs, sat in the Parliament—a powerful person. Once there was a young violinist who created a great furor of popular applause. A rival who was jealous spread an ugly rumor that he was not really great, that it was an extraordinary Stradivarius he played upon that made those moving tones that captivated the audiences. One night in London the violinist played his whole program without leaving the platform and more than ordinarily stirred the great audience to thunderous applause; then he took the violin he had been playing on all the evening, smashed it into pieces across his knee, and threw it upon the floor. He said, "I will now play one number on my violin." His quality was in himself and not merely in an instrument that money could buy. Character does not depend on things that money can buy. Character is the result of wise choices. Life is a series of choices. Sunday morning—reading comics, listening to the radio or coming to church—when you decide to come to church it goes toward building your character.

2. Money cannot buy a happy home. We must grant that domestic trouble is often caused by lack in the home of the things that money can buy. We must grant that a child's chances for success are limited by the lack in the home of the things that money can buy. It is good to have radio, piano, refrigerators, etc. I knew a man who built a beautiful home, perhaps the most beautiful in the island. He has all the modern conveniences in the house—people came to see it. He invested all his money. Yes, it is good to have a lot of comforts

and luxuries in the home. But can you tell where the greatest wreckage of family life appears? Do you suppose it is found among the poor, the middle-class people or among the rich? You can have all the modern conveniences and appliances in the home but if you do not have the things that money cannot buy, the chances for the home to go on the rock are very great. What are they? Love and affection. In the long run, it is the things that money cannot buy that determine what the family will really be. There is a family that is having domestic trouble all the time, unhappy, quarrels, because one member in that family is selfish and greedy and thinks and talks about money all the time. The other night, the lady in the home called me up and said to me, "Rev. Osumi, please come over to help us. We are in trouble again." She was in tears. You can equip a house with all the comforts and luxuries but you cannot make it a happy home without the things that money cannot buy. It is love and affection and mutual consideration that make a happy home.

3. Money cannot buy true happiness. We sometimes think that a successful man is one who has accumulated a lot of wealth and money. We sometimes think that a successful man is he who has a large bank account. Once three boys were bragging about the greatness of their dads. One said, "My dad draws a couple of lines, puts dots on them, calls it music, sends it away and gets $25 for it." Another said, "That's nothing. My dad scribbles a few lines, calls it poetry, sends it away and gets $50 dollars for it." The third said, "That's nothing. My dad scratches notes on a few sheets of paper, gets up and reads it off on Sunday, and it takes four men to bring in the money." Success is often defined in economic terms. We often delude ourselves in thinking that greatness lies in the accumulation of money, and wealth. Many people slave themselves to get money and die. They can't take the money with them. John Milton wrote *Paradise*

Lost, Paradise Regained. He was poor. Gave his life to a cause. Spent his sight on it for writing *Paradise Lost* for 10 pounds. Beethoven was a poor man who wrote the Ninth Symphony and got a meager sum of money. Spinoza, great philosopher, made a poor livelihood, polishing lenses. Louis XVI offered him pension if he would dedicate a book to him. He would not since he didn't favor Louis XVI and chose to polish lenses and be happy. Fosdick said, "The deepest hell one can fall into will be to have everything to live with and nothing to live for." Statistics of suicides show more suicides among the rich than among the poor.

4. Money cannot buy faith. Recently a man said to me, "Reverend, I am giving money because I want to go to heaven when I die." You can't buy the ticket to heaven with money. You can buy tickets to a concert, carnival or such things but not the ticket to heaven. Money cannot buy our salvation. Not very long ago, there was a mine disaster in Illinois. Gas explosion. Fume filled the passages. Miners were trapped. Facing almost certain death in the passages of the mines, the men scribbled little messages to their dear ones. Then they scrawled on the rough rock floor of the room that was to be their death chambers, the words: "Notes in pockets." The central word in these notes was "love." Well, take faith out of love and there is little, if anything, left. These men had faith to believe that rescue parties would come, no doubt too late for them, but not too late to read their notes and pass them on to those to whom they were addressed. One man wanted his wife to be sure to send the children to Sunday school. Perhaps he wanted them to have something of the faith he had which made him unafraid of death. Real faith makes us unafraid. We may be sitting pretty today but tomorrow we may be entirely in a different situation…sick, lose arms or legs, sight. You can't buy that kind of faith with money. You can't nurture it on just one day, Sunday.

Conclusion: We live in a money-minded world and tend to think money can buy anything and money is everything. Some people are willing to barter their soul for money. It is good to check once in a while to be sure we have not lost the things we cannot buy with money…character, a happy home, true happiness, faith. These are the supreme values of life. These are the things that really make up life. We must be sure that we are centering our life in the things that money cannot buy. It is good to have money and the things that money can buy but it is good to check up once in a while to be sure we have not lost the things that money cannot buy.

Remember Who You Are
Nuʻuanu Congregational Church, 1970

There was a woman who had seven children. She was a good mother. She was not an educated woman, but she knew a great deal about psychology. Always when her children left the home to go for a visit or out to play with the other children, she followed them to the door and with a little pat of love for each one, she would say, "Now, children, remember who you are." There is an excellent bit of practical psychology in this mother's reminder to her children. As her children went out to meet life, she wanted them to remember their high calling of self-respect.

A young man was leaving home for college in a faraway city. Before he left home, he had expected his father to give him a long lecture about what his conduct should be…about how he should behave in the far city…about how he should stay away from the temptations of the city. To his surprise, his father said, "Whatever happens, I want you to know that your mother and I trust you." What an inspiration and help are those who expect only the best from others. Most likely the young man will not betray the trust placed upon him by his parents.

Human nature responds to responsibility and trust. We want to be trusted. We want to be depended upon. We want to be worthwhile. Give a man a confidence to prove true to and he will not want to be a traitor. He feels he cannot be a traitor without being false to himself. We need to be reminded who we are. We need to be reminded more than threatened with punishment if we fail. Here many parents make a mistake. They threaten their children with punishments. A far better and more effective way will be to trust them—to give them a responsibility to live up to. Good living that springs from fear of punishment is not real goodness. It is expediency.

We are all victims of a kind of mild amnesia. We forget who we are. We forget our identity. We need to discover ourselves. First of all, we do well to remember that we are human beings. If that sounds very elementary, please remember that a great number of people forget that. Too many people merely exist on the animal level. Too many people live with the philosophy, "Eat, drink and be merry for tomorrow you may die." Too many people live lives that are no different from animals.

We are not just beings. We are human beings. A mule is an animal. However low the plane to which we may have gravitated, we are still human beings. God made man a little lower than angels and has crowned him with glory and honor. Those who have allowed themselves to gravitate to the animal level need to be aroused from their amnesia. They need to remember who they are.

Again, we do well to remember that we are different from other human beings. You are you. No other person is exactly like you. No two human beings are exactly alike. Thank God we are created differently. Suppose all of us were exactly alike. That wouldn't be funny—that would be tragic. There are two twin brothers—both are doctors. They look alike. I often mistake one for the other. But upon close examination they are different. Each human has a personality all his own. We must retain our own personality and develop it to the highest extent.

Some time ago there was a newspaper article about a victim of amnesia. He had forgotten who he was. His parents had given him up as dead. His own life had become a hopeless thing. But one day suddenly he came to himself, and in unutterable joy he rushed to the telephone and called home, "Father! This is George. Your son George. I've just remembered who I am. I'm coming home."

There is a romantic story. A man wandered away from home. He forgot who he was. He found a job on a farm. Then he fell in love with the country schoolteacher. She refused to marry him, a man who didn't know who he was. Then one day the teacher had a severe automobile accident. She needed a delicate operation to remove a concussion. He was shocked with fear that she might die. Suddenly he realized who he was. He was a doctor. He shouted, "Now I remember who I am. I have done many such operations. I can save her."

Well, friends, take a look at yourself. Are you the kind of person you want to be? Are you the kind of man or woman your family wants you to be? Are you the kind of person God intended you to be when he sent you to live on earth? ✖

God in the Desert

Nuʻuanu Congregational Church, 1972

The subject of my sermon this morning was taken from the title of my booklet, which I published quite some time ago. During World War II, I served as minister in a relocation center in Arizona. The relocation center was in the desert. I am sure of what happened after the Pearl Harbor attack by Japanese planes. All the Japanese people on the West Coast were forcefully evacuated and placed in concentration camps (which are euphemistically called "relocation centers"). They had to leave practically everything behind—their homes, farms, businesses, cars, etc. One of the girls who used to come to our church wrote (she was writing about her experience of coming to the desert camp on a bus with other evacuees):

"On our way to Arizona in the train and in the bus, I became so lost that I almost lost God. I still remember that day as we were coming in that old bus across the desert; I looked up into the skies and said to myself, 'This is a God-forsaken country. Even God does not exist here.' Now I realize that God had been there all the time."

We find God in life's lovely experiences. We sing the doxology, "Praise God from whom all blessings flow." That is where we find him—in our blessings. But when darkness comes, when disaster strikes, we tend to lose sight of God and cry, "Where is God?"

Last Thursday morning, the *Honolulu Advertiser* carried a large picture of a man—an Iranian, carrying the dead body of his daughter taken from the rubble in the quake-stricken village of Shiraz. He seemed to be in a daze. Anguish and grief were written on his face. He lost all seven members of his family in the Monday earthquake. He could very well say, "Where is God?" One Englishman said, "I don't know what I believe, but I don't believe all this God is love stuff. I have been in two world wars. I have been unemployed 18 months on end.

I have seen my wife die of cancer. Now I am waiting for the atom bomb to fall. All that stuff about God is no help."

Well, did you ever feel like that? Did you ever find yourself in the desert? I am sure you know the story of Moses. Moses fled from Egypt. In anger, he killed an Egyptian taskmaster who was beating an Israelite. He escaped into the desert and became a shepherd. One day, while he was leading his flock in the desert, he heard the divine voice say, "The place where on thou standest is holy ground." He was in an unpromising place—in the desert, but now was told that that was holy ground.

Helen Keller did that. She was deaf, mute and blind and yet she was able to say, "I thank God for my handicaps for through them I have found myself, my work and my God." Now what made Moses discover holy ground in the desert? He saw his people cruelly and unjustly treated—treated as slaves. And he couldn't stand it. He had been brought up as the son of Pharaoh's daughter, living a soft life, a playboy at the royal court. As he grew up, he became more concerned about the plight of his people. One day, he saw a Hebrew slave beaten by an Egyptian taskmaster. He was so mad that he killed the taskmaster. He was no longer a playboy. He identified himself with the enslaved people, organized them, marched with them and led them from their bondage. "Let my people go." Martin Luther said, "When I am angry, I preach well and pray better." William Ollery Channing, the great preacher in New England said, "Ordinarily I weigh 120 pounds, but when I am mad I weigh a ton." When Jesus saw a deed of mercy held up by a ceremonial triviality, he "looked round about on them with anger." When Jesus saw little children being roughly brushed aside, he was "moved with indignation." When you see an act of injustice, when you see some evil in society, when you see something intolerably wrong, you ought to get angry. I would go so far as to say that you are not a Christian of you don't get angry.

Let us look at our world. It is hard to find God here. There are evils in our society. The other day, a gambler was killed in cold blood apparently by his fellow gamblers.

Gambling is a constant menace to society. There is the wide and prevalent use of drugs, especially by youth. There is the problem of poverty. In the midst of plenty and affluence we find ghettos and pockets of poverty. Another great social evil is racism. There is the problem of war and peace.

All is not well in our society. We can at least quit our moral apathy and wake up to the momentous issues in our community, our city, our nation and the world. Dietrich Bonhoeffer, the great German religious leader, was killed in a concentration camp by Hitler. His writings are being widely read by religious thinkers of the world. He wrote about the "worldliness" of God and the worldliness of discipleship. He argued that God is not a religious God preoccupied with "religious" ceremonies, but a God who is passionately involved in the agony and suffering of the world. He argued that the supernatural is found in the natural, the holy in the profane and the revelation in the rational.

In his encounter with right against wrong, in his justification for his people's sake, Moses came face to face with God. We often talk of God in terms of love, beauty and goodness so that when we face a situation in our personal experience or in the world at large, where love, beauty, goodness are absent, we lose our sense of God. "Where is He?" we ask. In days like these, we need God who encounters us in the desert. Soft occasions do not bring out the deepest in a man—never! Rather in formidable hours when loyalty to the right means the risk of everything, perhaps life itself, when we come to have our profoundest religious insights. The great prophet Isaiah encountered God in Babylon with his exiled people. Job, losing his family in calamities and himself afflicted with a terrible disease, says, "I have heard of Thee by the hearing of the ear, but now mine eye seeth Thee."

An alcoholic writes, "In the depths of my suffering I came to believe, to believe that there was a power greater than myself that could help me—to believe that because of that power, God, there was hope and help for me." So in the desert of her life, she found God.

Last Sunday in our adult class we reviewed a chapter in Dale Carnegie's book. The chapter was titled, "If You Have a Lemon, Make Lemonade." This advice was given by the founder of Sears, Roebuck and Co.

There is one illustration I would like to share with you. During the war, there was a woman whose husband was stationed at an army training camp near the Mojave Desert in California. She hated the place. When her husband was ordered out on maneuvers, she was left alone. The heat was unbearable—125 degrees in the shade of a cactus. Nobody to talk to but Mexicans and Indians and they couldn't speak English. The wind blew incessantly and the food she ate and the very air she breathed were filled with sand. She was utterly wretched. She felt sorry for herself. She wrote her parents that she was going to give up and come back home. Her father answered her letter with two lines: "Two men looked out from prison bars, one saw the mud, the other saw the stars." She decided to look for the stars. She made friends with the natives—showed interest in their weaving and pottery. They gave her presents. She studied the cactus, the yuccas and the Joshua trees. She learned about prairie dogs, watched for the desert sunsets. She was so excited by this new world that she wrote a book under the title, *Bright Ramparts*. "I had looked out for my self-created prison and found the stars." Nothing changed, but she herself changed and her whole world changed. She found God in the desert.

Your Style of Life

Nuʻuanu Congregational Church, 1972

About 10 days ago an interesting article appeared in the *Honolulu Advertiser*. It was about a former Honolulu lawyer. About a year ago he resigned from the law firm, started letting his hair and beard grow and moved his family to Switzerland. He was fully bearded; his hair was nearly shoulder length and wore mod clothing. He returned to Honolulu on a quick trip and he says of his new lifestyle, "I'd like to get on a box and stand in the middle of King Street and tell people how great it is." He was a lawyer in Honolulu and a politician. He says, "It's amazing how you can work hard and never think. Now, for the first time, I feel I'm a success. I'm finding out what life is and what love is and what people are." He is now teaching political science at the American College in Switzerland. He said of himself and his wife, "We spend a lot of time together. We shop together, we hike together and we ski together. We have a lot of time to learn to understand each other." He says, "There are greater values than making money." He feels that too many American businessmen, especially in business and the professions take their office troubles home with them, sip too many martinis in an attempt to forget those problems, and then become involved in arguments with their wives. He says, "I've got time now to live. That's really what success is."

Well, here is a story of a lawyer who is finding true happiness in a new style of life. Few of us can leave our work and go to Switzerland to live. Few of us want to let our hair and beard grow and wear mod clothes. I know I will never let my hair grow. But all of us want to live a truly satisfying and meaningful life. All of us want to find out what life is and what love is and what people are. All of us want to find values that are enriching and satisfying. All of us want to be a success in the true sense of the word. Whatever your style of life is, you want to be happy. In pursuing your style of life, you do well to take into consideration three things:

1. First of all, in your style of life, you must have a sense of what is important. One morning a mother tried to rouse her son from sleep. He was sleeping in an upstairs room. She called her son several times. After several unsuccessful attempts to rouse him, she said, "Aren't you ashamed, still to be in bed?" "Sure, Mom, but I'd rather be ashamed than get up." Without a sense of what is important it is simple forever to lie back and never get up. Without a sense of what is important it is simple forever to drift and live an empty and meaningless life. Christopher Columbus on his long journey to the New World made a single entry each night in his logbook: "This day we sailed westward, which is our course." He was uncertain about what lay ahead. He was faced with mutiny among his crew. He had to weather a heavy storm. Nevertheless, Columbus recorded, "This day we sailed westward." He found the New World because of his perseverance in what he believed important. A poet said, "A good man, struggling in his darkness, will always be aware of the true course." A man whose primary allegiance to God will always be "on course." He will put first things first. He will have a sense of what is important.

2. The second thing you must do as your pursue your style of life is to have a sense of responsibility. Some time ago there was a popular song with the words, "With A Little Bit of Luck." The song tells us of all the obligations that can be evaded, all the duties that can be dropped in someone else's lap "with a little bit of luck." But that is not a good philosophy of life. Man was given shoulders that he might carry a load. One evening a mother was going over a story with her little son. In the course of reading they came to the word "go." The boy said, "I know that word. It's come." Patiently his mother explained, "No, that's just the opposite." The boy couldn't understand "opposite of" and looked puzzled. So the mother said, "What do you do when

you don't come?" The boy responded immediately, "You get a spanking." Here was a boy who understood the meaning of responsibility. If you don't come, you get a spanking. If you don't fulfill your responsibilities, you face the consequences. I like this simple prayer:

> Lord, let me not die until I've done for Thee
> My earthly work, whatever it may be.
> Call me not hence with mission unfilled;
> Let me not leave my space of ground untilled;
> Impress this truth upon me that not one
> Can do my portion that I leave undone."

Each of us has a job to do. Each of us has been given the dignity of duty and the privilege of responsibility. This is what the Bible means when it says that man has been created in the image of God. The likeness of man to his Maker is revealed in every act of responsible decision, in every commitment honored, in every obligation followed to its conclusion.

3. The third thing you must do in your style of life is to have a sense of purpose. Some time ago a young man came to see me in my office. He was shabbily dressed. His hair was not combed—bushy and long. He looked as though he had not had a bath for some time. All the time he was talking to me, he was scratching himself. He had no job, no money. He told me that he had only 25 cents in his pocket. He had been sleeping on the beach and in the park. The tragedy of our modern life is that there are so many young people who are leading a meaningless existence. They are living an endless round of nothingness. This afternoon I will be attending the Annual Meeting of the Hawai'i Council of Churches. Instead of the usual program, all the delegates will see the Waikiki Ministry in action. The announcement says, "Following a brief business session, we will embark on a 'Jungle Safari.'" The tragedy of Waikiki is that so many young people are lost in the jungle, living aimlessly,

many of them addicted to drugs. There are so many aimless people roaming on the face of the earth. This is the sickness of our time. This is the malady of our generation. What flattens life for millions of people is its meaninglessness, its emptiness. Some are busy, going from place to place, but in Shakespeare's words, "All sound and fury, signifying nothing." Dr. E. Stanley Jones, after a preaching mission in the colleges and universities, said he believed the present generation of American youth is the finest the country had produced. They are taller in body, better trained in mind, more wholesome in attitude; but they lack one thing: a sense of mission, no great compelling purposes to lift them to their feet. Sometimes people say that they are going to pieces. Not long ago, a woman said to me, "Rev. Osumi, I am going to pieces." Life can go all to pieces in aimlessness. What we need in our lives is some master passion, some supreme devotion to hold our scattered lives together.

Part Three

TODAY'S THOUGHT

Today's Thought

Here are a few commandments for parents: 1. Give your children the support of love and confidence, appreciation of the individuality of each. 2. Give your children a share in the tasks, plans and activities of the home. 3. Look for good which you can praise rather than faults which you must condemn.

Rev. Osumi

Rev. Paul S. Osumi,
Nuuanu Congregational
Church.

Today's Thought

When Handel composed his famous oratorio, "The Messiah," he was in trouble. He was 56 years old and penniless. He had suffered a stroke two years before, and was partially paralyzed. Most of the music critics were against him. But out of his deep despair he wrote the glorious music.

Rev. Osumi

Rev. Paul S. Osumi,
Nuuanu Congregational
Church.

Today's Thought

My father wrote the inspirational daily sayings column Today's Thought for the *Honolulu Advertiser* from 1957 to 1993. Today's Thought also appeared in the *Hawaii Hochi* and the *Fairbanks Daily News-Miner* in Nome, Alaska. Numerous people I have met over the years mentioned they read my father's Today's Thought in the *Honolulu Advertiser*. They said the Today's Thoughts gave them something to look forward to in the newspaper each day. Many clipped their favorite Today's Thought and taped it to their refrigerator, mirror, office desk or wall, or kept it in their wallet or purse. These nuggets of wisdom provided people with insight and inspiration to live a happy and meaningful life. Selected Today's Thoughts from more than 35 years of published columns follow.

Is God the Universal Father?

The great tragedy of the modern age is that we have not grown. We remain cliff dwellers in an age when we should be citizens of the planet. We are still too narrow and small to embrace the world in our hearts. "My country is the world.... My native land is mother earth, and all men are my kin."

What Do We Live For?

Profit motive dominates the lives of many. With many Christians, money talks. The lure of personal profit is stronger than the lure of common good. We must decide what we are going to live for. If it is for money and possessions, we take our stand with those who live for the things that pass. If we are to live to make a life for ourselves and others, then we take our stand with the high souls of the ages.

Feeling Secure in an Insecure World

We are living in a troubled and uncertain world. The things we thought secure are tumbling down. Many people are suffering from the feeling of insecurity and uncertainty. We have lost the grand assurance that God is in His heaven and all is well with the world. Once a professor of philosophy at Yale University said, "We must get God back into the universe." What is more important is to find a place for Him in the human soul.

Activity Without Objective

We live in an age of speed. We move and do things fast. There are many people who keep themselves very busy…and yet do nothing. "Nothing," said Carlyle, "is more terrible than activity without insight." The tragedy of life is meaningless activity without objective. Blessed is the man whose activity is directed by some great purpose. The man who has not learned to direct his energies with heavenly wisdom is wasting his life in empty motions.

What Makes the Difference?

Once two men walked in a rose garden. One of them explained, "My, aren't these roses beautiful?" But the other said disgustingly, "Oh, they are full of thorns." One saw the beautiful roses but the other saw nothing but thorns. They walked in the same garden, saw the same thing. But one saw beauty and the other ugliness. It is the attitudes they have toward life that makes people see things differently.

Cost of a Happy Marriage

The mere fact that a couple gets happily married doesn't mean they are going to be happy. In order to possess the joy and happiness of marriage, the couple must pay a price in terms of courtesy, consideration and respect. We cannot have anything worthwhile without paying the price. Happiness in marriage has a price tag.

Reason for Marital Failure

A husband and wife were having trouble. Each blamed the other for the stained relationship and their marital failure. Neither was willing to be sufficiently honest to say, "The neglect is mine. I am at fault." Such trouble cannot be resolved until both sides are willing to admit their guilt.

Couple Separation

A couple sought a minister for counseling. Their home had been a happy one for a few years, and then each became a slave to a schedule. The pressure of the schedule slowly but surely forced them apart. Before long, they were living in separate worlds. It is tragic how we neglect our loved ones in our own homes.

Mother's Children Prayer

A mother prayed, "Help me treat my children as of their own age, but let me not exact of them the judgment and conventions of adults. Allow me not to rob them of the opportunities to wait upon them, to think, to choose and to make decisions. Fit me to be loved and imitated by children."

Marriage Priorities

There are men to whom the skill of their golf game has become of such vital importance that it absorbs all energy they should be devoting to their children, their marriage, their church. There are women to whom social affairs have become so important that the deep meaning of marriage and family escapes them altogether.

What's Missing?

A home may lack luxuries such as a television, washing machine or comforting parlor set, but let it lack love and all the luxuries in the world cannot make it a real home. A person may lack education and even refinement, but let him lack integrity and all the education in the world cannot make up for that essential lack.

Show Appreciation

How many people try to make up with flowers, tears and belated words of appreciation for what they failed to do and say when someone was alive? Why not express your love and appreciation when they are yet alive?

Expectation After Death

A man who was dying asked what the future life would be like. Just then the doctor heard his dog, which had followed him to the house, scratching at the door. He told the man, "My dog knows nothing of what is happening behind the door, but merely wants to be with his master. You don't know what lies behind the door, but you can be sure that your Master is there."

Truly Forgiving?

A man was dying. He was asked to become reconciled to a neighbor with whom he had quarreled. He agreed and the neighbor was brought in. They shook hands and expressed mutual forgiveness. As the neighbor was about to go, the sick man said, "But remember, if I get well this doesn't count." How forgiving we are at times.

After Death

Death is one experience we all share in common. No insulation against death has been found, but we usually do not think about death until it comes into our home and takes away someone who is dear to us. Let us believe that at the end of life there are open doors. Let us believe in God, whose will it is that none of us shall be lost.

Acceptance Alternative

A father and mother learned that their teenage son was going blind. The boy's father said, "We have three choices. We can curse life for doing this to us and express our grief and rage. Or we can grit our teeth and endure it. Or we can accept it. The first alternative is useless. The second is sterile and exhausting. The third way is the only way."

Life's Decision

Shakespeare, in his play *Julius Caesar,* has Cassius say, "The fault, dear Brutus, is not in our stars, but in ourselves." It is not fate that decides your fortune or misfortune. You are not at the mercy of circumstances. You can decide. It is not what life brings to you, but what you do with what life brings to you that decides your life.

Life's Arithmetic

A man said, "Life is a lot like a kid's problem in arithmetic. We get all mixed up." We often make mistakes in life's arithmetic. We keep adding and multiplying life's possessions when we ought to be dividing them among others. We keep on subtracting from the list of people we should care about when we ought to be adding to the list.

Value in Life's Meaning

We are often so busy making a living, we forget to make a life. Our love of things often blinds us to spiritual realities. We fuss over petty affairs. We jostle impatiently for possessions or some empty honor, while the most worthwhile things in life are lost. We often lose sight of everything but wealth.

Forget the Past

A man asks, "I have sold my business. Do you think I have done the right thing?" One of the hardest things most of us have to learn is to make decisions and then stop second guessing. You do something, and then spend a sleepless night wishing you hadn't. What's done is done. Crying over spilt milk is foolish. Forget the past and face the future.

Learn to Listen

A man in trouble said to his minister, "Thank you very much. You have helped me greatly." Yet the minister had done nothing except to listen. If we are to do well in this world, we must learn to listen. In times of great stress, words are often futile. Often the only comfort and help we can give our friends in sorrow is to be silent and listen.

Aging Benefits

A wise man said, "Why be happy on New Year's Day? Remember you are one year nearer to your grave." Well, that is one way of looking at life. We are getting older, to be sure, but we are also getting wiser, more experienced, more mature in our thinking and more able to see deeper meaning in life. We are happy as we face the New Year because the best of life is yet to be.

Pain and Suffering

A young man wrote, "If there is a good God, why does he allow so much pain and suffering in the world?" But what is he asking for? A world where there is nothing but ease, pleasure and happiness? Everything worthwhile in life has to come out of a background of struggle against obstacles. Pain and suffering have a positive role in life.

Finding Happiness

A preacher asked those in his congregation who wanted to go to heaven to stand up. All rose but one man. Then he asked who wanted to go to hell to stand up. Nobody rose. The puzzled parson asked the non-cooperative man where he wanted to go. He replied, "Nowhere, I like it here." If we can't find happiness where we are, we are likely not to find it anywhere.

Disappointments in Life

A young man wrote: "Everything has gone wrong with me." Yes, in life things do go wrong. A man who dreamed of becoming a physician is now a bookkeeper. A couple that dreamed of a beautiful home now lives in a tiny apartment. A businessman who had big plans has a small store. In life we cannot always realize our ambitions. We must make the best of what life brings.

Suffering Acceptance

We sometimes indulge in self-pity by thinking that disappointments, failures, heartaches and tragedies are peculiar to us. But they are common lot of us all. We are not singled out for an undue share of life's woes. Suffering is a principle of life itself; as long as we live in this world we all have to suffer.

Work Advice

A mother gave this priceless advice to her son, who was about to start a job: "John, remember, it is not how much you get from your job that is important. It is how much you can put into it that counts." Later the son became a successful and greatly revered businessman. He said through the years he had never forgotten his mother's advice.

Living Alone

Many people try to run away from their inner loneliness. They do not know how to be alone. They do anything to escape from being alone. They are always on the go, they are always doing something. To live meaningful, we must master one of the fine arts of life—learning to be alone without being lonely. We must learn to live with ourselves.

The Good Life

A few years ago *Life* magazine had a special issue on "The Good Life." It was shown that we have in America wonderful resources of the good life, including machines and mechanical appliances. But we must remember that the good life is more than things. It is primarily a life of commitment to great purpose of mind and heart.

Few Great Words

It is said a parrot can learn 200 to 300 words; a bright six-year-old knows about 2,000 to 3,000 words; an ordinary person, 35,000 to 70,000 words. But the really important thing in life is not how many words we know, but how well we know a few great words. How well do you know great words such as faith, hope and love?

Criticism by Others

Someone said, "Pay no attention to ill-natured remarks about you. Simply live, thinking that nobody will believe them." No one can avoid the criticism of others. Even Lincoln was called "a monster in human form—an ape man." Has someone said ugly things about you? Have a heart big enough to overlook the abuses and slander.

Life's Goodness

During a particularly bad sales slump, a manager talked to a group of his salesmen. Placing a black spot on a large white screen, he asked his men what they saw. All replied, "A black spot". The manager said, "Can't any of you see the large white surface?" We need to pay less attention to life's frustrations and more to life's goodness.

Participate in Life

Our generation enjoys watching sports and games. Someone called it the disease of our time and named it "spectatorities." Crowds cheer at football games and baseball games, horse races, car races. Throngs fill movie theaters. The eyes of families are glued to television screens in the evening. It is better to actively participate in recreation than to merely see others perform. It is better to take an active part in life than to watch it.

Stepping Forward

A Marine officer, needing three men for a dangerous mission, asked for volunteers. He said to the platoon, "I am going to turn my back and give three men the opportunity to move forward one step." He turned around for a few minutes, then faced the ranks again. A look of irritation crept over his face. He didn't see the three men. Then the sergeant explained, "Sir, the entire platoon has stepped forward."

Money: Good or Evil

Money can be either a blessing or a curse. The Bible does not say, "Money is the root of all evil," but it does say, "The love of money is the root of all evil." Money in itself is neutral, and is neither good nor bad. We make it good or bad by the way we use it. We must use it to benefit not only ourselves, but our society.

Personal Treasures

In life there are many kinds of treasures, and they are not all made of silver and gold. When you find a friend, you find a treasure. When you find goodness anywhere, you find a treasure. The finest possessions in life are personal treasures of kindness, joy, peace of mind, faith and love.

Road of Life

Every man travels a winding, dusty road. Every now and then he comes to new sights and new grandeur. But sooner or later every road of life tumbles down into a valley where life becomes difficult with suffering and pain and adversity. Rich and poor, young and old, wise and unwise all have to pass through it.

Brighten Your Life

Here are eight steps to brighten your life:
1. Begin the day in a cheerful mood.
2. Try smiling at others.
3. Count your blessings.
4. Live life one day at the time.
5. Give some friends a phone call or a letter.
6. Be a happy person. See the bright side of life.
7. Do a good deed. Give something good to a loved one.
8. Give of yourself. Offer your service to a church or a hospital.

—Dr. Alfred A. Montapert

Are You Miserable?

There are 11 ways to be miserable:
1. Use "I" as often as possible.
2. Be sensitive to slight.
3. Be jealous and envious.
4. Think only about yourself.
5. Talk only about yourself.
6. Trust no one.
7. Never forget criticism.
8. Expect to be appreciated.
9. Be suspicious.
10. Listen to what others say of you.
11. Look for faults in others.

Service Others

In an old Persian legend, a father leaves his son a mirror and goes on a long journey. When he returns, he discovers his son has starved to death looking at himself. If a person constantly looks at himself alone, he is sure to starve himself emotionally and spiritually. We must throw away our mirrors and forget ourselves in service to others.

Understanding Others

While we live our short life on this earth, we come into contact with all sorts of people—people of different colors, shapes, sizes and ways of life. The problem is: What shall be the basis of our relationship with them? Some seek isolation. Some build a wall of prejudice. Life, however, is deepest and richest when we seek to love and understand our neighbors.

Honesty

An interesting cartoon shows a merchant weighing a dressed chicken. Unseen by the woman customer, he has his finger pressing down the scale. Unseen by the merchant, the woman has a finger under the scale pushing up. The cartoon does not show what the outcome was. It doesn't pay to cheat and deceive. Honesty is the best policy.

Live Each Day

Death may come to us suddenly at any time. It behooves all of us to live each day as if it were the only day we had. What if you are not here tomorrow? It behooves all of us to live fully and make the most of each day as it comes.

Speech

A speaker sat down after making a long, wordy speech and remarked, "I couldn't have said less, unless I had said more." In a speech it is better to be relevant and concise than long and rambling. It is better to be truthful than deceitful. It is better to say what we mean and mean what we say.

Good Health

We must exercise common sense in matters of proper diet, rest, exercise, sunshine and weight. It is for us to observe the rules of good health. You have only one body that is irreplaceable.

Laugh Away Troubles

The famous clown Girmaldi was privately a miserable man. Like many of us, he had a hard time getting along with himself. He finally sought a counselor, asking for some rare talisman that might dispel his inward wretchedness. The counselor told him to go and listen to a famous clown by the name Girmaldi and he would laugh away his troubles. "Alas," said the luckless clown, "I am Girmaldi."

What's Important

A woman writes, "My husband and I don't have big fights, but we quarrel over little things all the time." People who are fond of each other often allow themselves to quarrel over little things. They elect to be miserable by indulging in trivial bickering. Why not keep your eyes fixed upon important matters and overlook the trifles?

Do Our Best

A young man lamented, "Some people have all the breaks and I have none." Yes, it is true some people have so much in the way of talent, ability and material resources. None of the good things of life seem to come our way. But nothing is to be gained by envy of what other people have. With God's help we must do the best with what we have.

Discipline

John Miller wrote, "There is not a thing in the world of more grave and urgent importance, throughout the whole life of a man, than discipline." A swimmer becomes a champion as he disciplines himself rigorously day after day. The surgeon becomes skillful in surgery through discipline. Acceptance of discipline is the price of excellence in any field.

Sitting Still

We live a fast life nowadays. We leap out of bed, gulp down coffee, whiz into town, dash to the office and tear for home. Our life is one of anxiety, impatience, restlessness and tension. No wonder people have ulcers, breakdowns and heart attacks. Pascal was right when he said, "All the troubles of man come from his not knowing how to sit still."

To Live Happily

Many people are miserable because they are shut up as prisoners in the solitary confinement of their cells. Their interest and attention are focused on themselves. The woes and sorrows of others are not their concern. They are nothing but their own troubles. To live happily, we must get out of ourselves and into the lives of others.

Carrying Double Load

In life there are two sets of facts—one we can control, the other beyond our control. If we do not draw a distinction between the things we are responsible for and things we are not, we pile on ourselves a load too heavy to bear. Our business is to do our job the best way we know how and trust God for the rest. Why carry the double load?

Things to Do?

If a man begins his day wondering what to do with himself, he is already as good as dead. But the man who really lives has more to do than he can accomplish. For such a man, retirement means nothing. Recently a man of 85 corrected the proofs of his books on the day of his death.

Strive for a Goal

Hugh Anderson Moran's book, *Makers of America*, is a study of the lives of 63 people elected to the American Hall of Fame. The author concludes, "The development of a dominant purpose seems to be the essential requisite of a successful life." To succeed in any endeavor, one must set up a goal and persistently strive to reach it.

Keep Trying

In life we cannot always realize our ambition. Our plan is often upset and our dream shattered. Few men and women are now doing what they first wanted to do. It takes courage to take a broken plan and make a great thing of it. Don't hold a grudge against life if you can't have your own way. Take a second choice and make the best of it.

End of the Rope?

A man said to a minister, "I have come to the end of my rope. There is only one way out. I am going to end it all." The minister took him to visit a hospital. There they met about 30 incurables who seemed radiant and happy. The desperate man changed his mind and said, "I will find my way." The incurables had cured him.

Relationship Gap

We hear of the "generation gap" nowadays. But age is not the only thing that separates people. There may be a gap between husband and wife, between brother and sister, between friend and friend. Feelings of love may be there but remain unexpressed. People can be close to each other physically but unable to reach each other.

Marriage Relationship

A woman said to a minister, "My husband has told me he doesn't love me anymore and that he is in love with another woman. I've kept his home neat and clean, given him good meals and kept his clothes in order." The minister asked her, "Did you show interest in his work? Did you give him companionship, understanding and sympathy, as well as housekeeping?"

Problem with Ourselves

A man would say, "If I had a better break, I would have succeeded." It is difficult for us to realize our worst enemy is within us. It is much easier to believe that somewhere outside us lay the obstacles, either in circumstances or in people. But there is no victory until we conquer ourselves.

Robert Louis Stevenson's Prayer

On Sunday evening just before his death, Robert Louis Stevenson read a new prayer he had written: "Go with each of us to rest…and when the day returns…call us up with morning faces and morning hearts, eager to labor, happy, if happiness shall be our portion…and if the day be marked for sorrow, strong to endure it."

Bury Failures and Mistakes

Haunting memories often arise to disturb our peace of mind. There are certain deeds of ours of which we are ashamed. Angry words were spoken for which we are sorry. There were opportunities we failed to grasp. But what is done is done. We must bury our failures and mistakes in the cemetery of the forgotten.

Life's Question

The famous second-century theologian Tertullian once condemned the sharp business practices of a friend. The friend retorted, "But I have to live." Tertullian immediately responded to his friend, "Why?" The adequacy and power of our lives depend heavily upon the adequacy and our power of our reasons for living. We do well to ponder the question, "Why do I live?"

Talking Too Much?

Someone said, "Keep skid chains on your tongue, always say less than you think." This is a good rule. We often make blunders by talking too much. How often we regret that we have said! But our spoken words, like a spent arrow, do not come back. It is better to restrain our speech than to be sorry afterward for our garrulity.

Eternal Life

Someone said, "While we are on the way to heaven, we have heaven on the way." Eternal life is not something to be obtained when we die; it is something to be accepted now. Of course, we believe in life after death. But we who live in fellowship with God have no fear of death, for we have experienced eternal life here and now.

Helping Others

Our life on this earth is very brief. Like a flicker of light, it is blown out before we know it. There is no time in it to fuss, fret or fume over trifles. There is nothing worthwhile in it except to be kind and helpful to our fellow men. There is no real happiness in it except to be generous and give freely to help our burdened friends.

Getting Along

To be happy in life, we must overcome our everyday difficulty of getting along with others. Out friendships are often broken by a careless word, an uprush of temper, a gesture of indifference, a slight difference of opinion. Always everywhere there is the problem of getting along with people.

Accepting Guilt

We tend to accuse others of bringing about the unfortunate circumstances in which we find ourselves. We tend to look for scapegoats. Like children escaping punishment, we say, "He made me do it." We blame everything and everybody for our plight except ourselves. We must have courage to confront ourselves and say, "I, too, am guilty."

Saying "No"

The two-letter word "NO" has to be said often to keep our life sane and simple. Some people cannot utter this little word and keep on accepting requests even though they are already loaded with other duties, or keep on buying things even though they don't need them. It is foolish to agree just to be agreeable. We must have the courage to say no and stick to it.

State of Mind

Someone said, "Youth is not a time of life...it is a state of mind. Nobody grows old merely by living a number of years. People grow old by losing their ideals. We are as young as our faith, as old as our doubts; as young as our confidence, as old as our fears; as young as our hope, as old as our despair.

Word "Empathy"

Empathy is good word to add to your vocabulary. It means putting oneself in another's place. It goes beyond sympathy, which means feeling sorry for others. Empathy represents that insight whereby we enter into another's experience completely so that we actually identify ourselves with him and see life from his own mind and being.

Taking Part

A man described how he avoided getting involved in squabbles: "I just put myself in neutral and take it easy." But, the trouble with the world is that too many people have put themselves in neutral. They take no part in the struggle of right against evil. We must not be neutral in battles for civic decency, human rights, brotherhood and peace.

Depressed and Lonely

Have you lost your dearest one and you feel depressed and lonely? Then do not spend all your time on the blessed memories of the past and live a closeted life. Open your life to new friendships and new interests. Find someone or some interest to even partially replace the emptiness, the loss of your loved one has wrought.

Solitude

We often become exhausted by our frantic, furious and noisy living. We desperately need solitude. Even 15 minutes spent daily in silence and meditations will give meaning and depth to our life. Calmness of spirit and serenity of outlook are nourished in the silences.

Living to the Fullest

Someone said, "Life is the quality of being responsive to the things about us. So, greet the morning with an expectant spirit. Reach out for all the good things that come within our grasp. Quicken your senses to establish contact as though you believed in God and shared his love. Live all your life."

Child's Interdependence

One of the greatest moments in the life of every mother is to watch her son or daughter trudging off alone on the first day of school. The mother's eyes may be misty with tears, but she knows her child must begin to become dependent and learn to adjust to others and not become completely dependent on the parents.

What is Life

To eat and drink and sleep; to seek the things that do not last; to live just for physical kicks and thrills—this is not life. To know the love of wives, children and friends; to give and forgive and forget; to look up not down; and to lend a hand to lift the burden of our fellows—this is life.

Way to Look at Things

We do not need to be embittered because others are spiteful, forgetful, neglectful or impossibly difficult. Why not assign their bad dispositions to poor health, indigestion or some frustration or disappointment? Such an attitude would sweeten our relationship with them and make us all happier and better.

Why Worry?

We spend many sleepless nights worrying about a future event. But, seldom does anything happen as we imagine it. Worry is interest paid in advance. It is a total loss. It spoils tomorrow before tomorrow arrives. It makes us tried and exhausted before the day begins.

Live Today

We can do anything for one day. Let us forget yesterday with its mistakes and failure. Let us not waste our time thinking of tomorrow's burdens. For one day, let us be happy. For one day, let us be kind, be cheerful, find no fault and live our best—today.

Do Good Now

Our life on this earth is short and our years pass by quickly. We do need to heed what a wise man said: "We have to do all the good we can as we go along, because if we don't our best years will be done for good or our fingers will get too stiff to open generously. We had better make hay while the sun shines, and live while we are alive."

Smile

When you feel the corners of your mouth turning down, turn them up instead. Dark and gloomy feelings thrive on downturned lips, and the only things that can pass between them are words better left unsaid. Smile and see how quickly your miseries vanish, how the cobwebs clear out of your mind, and how the whole world looks brighter.

Regrets

Some people make their lives miserable with their regrets. They brood over their past deeds. They say, "If only I had done that." Well, you didn't and that's that. It's no use crying over spilt milk. Let go of your regrets. Don't carry an unnecessary burden. Forget the past and face the future.

Money Cannot Buy

We often make the mistake of thinking that money is everything in life. But, there are things it cannot buy. Think of the free bounties of God's outdoor beauty: trees, flowers and sunshine. You cannot buy friendship, love, good character, a free conscience, a peace of mind or the forgiveness of God.

Great Garden

Here is a good garden formula: Plant five rows of peas—preparedness, promptness, perseverance, politeness and prayer; three rows of squash—squash gossip, squash indifference and squash criticism; five rows of lettuce—let us be faithful, unselfish, loyal, truthful and let us love one another; and one row of turnips—turn up for church!

Happy Thoughts

When we find ourselves restless and unable to fall asleep at night, why not put happy thoughts into our mind, instead of putting pills into our stomach. Why not ask ourselves, "What happy things have happened today?" Did we see a beautiful sunset or did we smell a fragrant rose? Did we do a good turn that wasn't discovered? Think happy thoughts.

Life Treasures

In life, there are many kinds of treasure and it is not all made of silver and gold. When you find a friend, you find a treasure. The finest possessions are not the material things of life, but the personal treasures of kindness, joy, peace of mind, faith and love.

Life's Battle

Life is so full of unpleasant things and hectic experiences that we want to get away from it all. Yes, life is hard and we become discouraged at times. We are tempted to run away from it. The way to escape is easy, but we must not take the easy way. We must struggle, fight and win the battle.

Life's Decisions

In life, we have to make decisions constantly. We must decide what we will be, what we will make of ourselves, whom we will marry and when. When our dreams are broken, we must decide what to do—give up or try again. When disaster overtakes us, we can go down in defeat or rise above it. After all, life is all decisions. You can choose your life.

Gratitude

It is said that a certain man always put on his spectacles when he was about to eat strawberries, so they would look bigger and more tempting. If we put on the spectacles of gratitude and appreciation, everything will look nicer and more beautiful. A sense of gratitude magnifies our common blessings. It will show us what a wonderful world is ours.

Sense of Humor

The feelings of some people are hurt easily. They are too sensitive and thin-skinned. They are wounded at the slightest provocation. They take innocent remarks as criticism. To save themselves from misery they must cultivate a sense of humor so they may laugh off real or imaginary slights.

Questions to Ask Ourselves

Here are a few questions we do well to ask ourselves. Do I lose my temper easily? Do I get blue and sulk when things don't go my way? Do I fuss about simple happenings? Am I a poor loser? Do I have constructive work to do day by day? Do I run away from difficulties? Have I practiced doing things I don't like to do?

Winning People

Here are the six rules for winning people to your side:
1. Treat everyone you meet as if he were important.
2. Be friendly.
3. Let other people do the talking; be a good listener.
4. Don't argue; you may win an argument but you will lose a friend.
5. Put yourself in the other fellow's shoes.
6. Practice finding the good in people.

Work at an Older Age

No man is too old to do his work. Life comes to its ripening in the 50s. A man should be able to do his best then. At 60 a man has made enough mistakes to make him wise. He should live better and do better work than ever before. And some of the best work is done in the 70s and 80s.

Life's Outlook

Do you know that as long as you don't despair or look upon life bitterly, things work out fairly well in end? Do you know that happiness is a perfume you cannot sprinkle on others without getting a few drops on yourself? Do you know that most people are lonely and many a stranger would be happy if you gave them a kind word and not a stony stare?

Developing More Than

Using our inventive genius, we have built a civilization that is nothing but complex implements. We can boast of clever gadgets, devices and appliances. It is good to build skyscrapers, but we must also come nearer to God. It is good to build huge bridges, but we must also build bridges into the lives of other nations.

Growing Old

Do you have symptoms of old age? You are growing old if you have lost the spirit of adventure and have stopped striving for new goals. You are growing old if you jog along in the old, familiar ruts. You are growing old if you play it safe and refuse to stick your neck out to fight for what is right.

Hurry and Worry

Two things mar our peace of mind and upset our lives—hurry and worry. The results of hurry are strain, jangled nerves, sleepless nights and upset stomachs. The cure is order, system and method. As for worry, it is due to too much imagination. It is fear in its subtlest shape. If a thing is inevitable, we must face it. If disaster looms, we must have courage to meet it.

Close Every Gate

A sign on a gate reads: "Please Shut This Gate." These four words are a good philosophy. We do well to learn to shut the gate on our mistakes grieves and grievances. We do well to let bygones be bygones. Don't double your load and shed needless tears by reliving the past. Learn to close every gate as you go along in life.

Higher Goals

A retired businessman was asked what he did in his spare time. He said, "When I get up in the morning I read the obituary column in the newspaper. If my name isn't there, I go back to sleep." This is true of a good many of us long before our time of retirement. We become satisfied just to be alive. No life needs be lived on a dead level. As human beings we must keep on aspiring to higher goals.

What We Have

We often give way to vain regrets and think we would be happier if we had a different choice. We might say, "If I had married someone else, or if I had followed some other line of work, how much better off I would be." It is better not to be an "iffer." It is folly to spend time in vain regrets. We must do our best with what we have.

Live a Wider Life

If you would, escape worry, keep your world large. Allow your sympathies to broaden. Be interested in causes that promote human welfare. Keep busy by doing things for others. Widen your scope in life.

Smile

Start your day with a smile. Greet everyone at the office with a pleasant smile. Start the day by spreading cheer and happiness. Give a smile to everyone. No one is properly clothed unless he wears a smile. Smile is a contagious thing. It is rest to the weary, daylight to the discouraged, sunshine to the sad and nature's best antidote for trouble.

Start a New Life

You cannot be happy within yourself if you hate yourself for what you are or for what you have done. You cannot be happy if you have stooped to the base and low, when you know you should have stood for the noble and high. You need not run forever from yourself or bear forever the burden of a bad conscience and a sense of guilt. With God's help you can make a new start and live a new life.

Ask Yourself

When evening comes it is good to review your day and ask yourself, "Have I been kind and thoughtful, or thoughtless? Have I kept an even temper, or have I lost my temper when things went wrong? Have I been pleasant, or grouchy? Have I done something creative and worthwhile, or have I wasted the day with petty things? Have I enlarged my mental horizon and expanded my personality?"

Maturity

Here are a few criteria for maturity:
1. The ability to deal constructively with reality.
2. The capacity to adapt to change.
3. Relative freedom from symptoms that are produced by tensions and anxieties.
4. The capacity to find more satisfaction in giving than receiving.
5. The capacity to relate to other people in a consistent manner.
6. The capacity to love.

Love People

Someone said, "We are created to love people and to use things. But the trouble is we reverse this order so we end up loving things and using people. We must learn to see people as people, not as things. We often commit the sin of dehumanizing people and using them as a means to an end. Let us always love people, not things."

Overwork

Many people commit the sin of overwork. The pressure is harder and the pace swifter than they should already allow themselves. They are always catching up with their work. They scarcely know their own children. Why drive yourself too hard? Why not slow down? Why not take time out occasionally and spend it with your family?

Needless Worry

We sometimes drive the car with the brakes on. "I smell burning brakes" is a remark that quickly makes us realize we had forgotten to release the handbrake. To worry is like driving a car with the brakes on. Many people work with low efficiency because their energy is consumed in needless worry.

Companionship

There are many lonely people who need to feel the warmth and joy of companionship. How often we hesitate to offer a friendly word, give a friendly smile or make a friendly gesture? We must always be alert to do the loving, friendly thing at the right time and where it is needed. We must be ready to offer a friendly word or smile.

Relaxation

The lunch hour can be a time for relaxation and a real break in the day's tensions. But, many run out, gulp down a sandwich and often coffee and rush back to the desk. Why not enjoy even the short time you have in a leisurely walk, in relaxing conversation with friends or in reading something that amuses you?

Forgiveness of God

The most powerful therapeutic idea in the world is the forgiveness of God. Thousands of people are sick because of their repressed guilt. Our usual advice to these people is "Forget it" or "Don't do it again." But such advice is no real help. What is needed is the assurance of the cleansing forgiveness of God.

God's Strength

It is natural for us to feel lonely when we are separated from our loved ones. Especially when our bonds are broken by death, we feel utterly lonely. Sometimes a bereaved and lonely person says, "Now I have nothing to live for." At such a time, instead of nursing our hurt and grief, we must look to God for strength to carry on.

Saving and Giving

A child's piggy bank is often found in the home. It is a device to teach the child thrift. A mother would say to her child, "Save your pennies. Put them in the piggy bank." It is important to train our children to save money, but it is also important to train them to give so they will derive pleasure in giving freely and generously something that is their own.

See Good Things

When things go wrong we need to remember the good things that are ours. There are things in life that makes us feel sorry for ourselves. But to dwell on them is to be unfair to ourselves. We must strike a balance. If we are honest about it we must admit the years have brought us more good than ill.

Write a Letter

The best time to write a letter is now. Thank you notes should not be postponed. Write them while the reason for gratitude is still fresh in your mind. Letters of congratulation should also be written on the spot. Never postpone writing to a friend who is ill. As soon as possible write to a friend who is ill. As soon as possible write to a friend who has suffered bereavement.

Going to Bed

There is an art in going to bed. The best way is to go to bed thankful for what the day has brought; conscious that you've hurt no one, that you've done what you should and a bit more, that you've made someone happy. Then you will sleep well and wake the next morning with a gallant spirit and a brave heart ready for whatever the day may bring.

Telling Jokes

Someone said, "Wit and humor at the other fellow's expense are rarely worth the effort, and may hurt where least expected." It is good to be witty and humorous. It is good to make others laugh. But, don't let others be the subject of your jokes. If you must tell jokes, let them be yourself and not about others.

Attitude

There are at least two attitudes to take toward any situation: One is negative, the other positive. One person, looking at a glass partially filled with water, remarks that the glass is half empty. Another person, looking at the same glass, remarks that it is half full. Each instance is the same, but the attitude is different.

Life's Ills

In life there is so much weighing us down, to depress our minds, to undermine our spirits—so many doubts, heartaches, regrets fears, worries and anxieties. In our moments of weakness, we hear the trumpets of defeat. But, thank God, the bells of joy ring in our hearts when we know that Christ can give us victory over all of life's ills.

Personal Prayer

Here is a good prayer: "God, keep me from chewing my pills. When life brings bitter experiences, help me to swallow them quickly. May I not add to their unpleasant taste by grumbling and complaining. Save me from the whining spirit that alienates my friends and makes me unfit for my duties. Keep me from being unhappy when I cannot have my own way."

God's Security

Life is uncertain and unstable. We can never tell what will happen to us today, tomorrow or next week. We are at the mercy of diseases, heart attacks, drunken drivers, accidents, earthquakes and tidal waves. Our apparent security is an illusion. Our only security is in God.

Accepting Criticisms

Someone wrote, "To be criticized, vilified and misunderstood is part of the penalty for leadership." Any person in a position of prominence must always keep in mind that if he is going to accomplish anything worthwhile, he must have courage and fortitude to stand against the abuse and criticisms of others.

Aging

When we retire and do nothing, our body system slows down and disintegrates. As a result, our life is short ended. In New England, the Yankee stronghold of America, clipper ships and whalers ran to India, China and Japan. There is an old saying as good today as ever: "It is better to wear out than rust out."

Exercise Regularly

"You're never too old to exercise." Exercise can be as strenuous as a game of tennis, as relaxing as gardening or as unorganized as an evening walk. What matters is that it must be regular. The results are improved muscle tone, better blood circulation and respiration, good appetite and digestion and relief from physical and mental tensions.

In God, Not Pills

There is an alarming increase in the sale of what are called "happiness pills." We swallow pills to pep us up, pills to take off weight and pills to calm us down. Thousands can't get to sleep without barbiturates or make it through the day without tranquilizers. We need faith—not pills, but in GOD.

State of Mind

If you think you are beaten, you are. If you think you dare not, you don't. If you like to win, but you think you can't, it's almost a cinch you won't. If you think you'll lose, you've lost. For out in the world you'll find success begins with a will. It's all in the state of mind.

God's Help

Do you sometimes say, "Today, I am down in the dumps"? You mean that you are in a low mood and that nothing goes right—everything is a source of annoyance. It may be that you are physically tired or emotionally fatigued. Why not rest awhile? Why not ask God to give you strength to pull yourself together?

Life's Worthwhile Things

All worthwhile things in life must be cultivated. If we don't take care of our garden, weeds grow. Flowers, fruits and vegetables require cultivation. So do our friendships. Family ties ought to be straightened. Old friendships ought to be deepened and new friendships formed. Let us remember that our friends are life's golden nuggets.

Pressure

There are many people who are working under pressure. They feel pressured with the thought that they don't have enough time. As the consequence, they do their work in a careless, slipshod manner. It is better to take our attention off the clock and the calendar, and concentrate on the quality of work done. We must learn to be thorough and efficient.

Work Positively

There are two ways in which we may do our work. We may take it as a necessary part of life and skimpily do the bare requirements. Thousands of people with their eyes on the clock are working this way. Another way is to look upon our work as something important and put all we have into it. In this way, we make our work a joy, rather than drudgery.

Distress to Blessing

In the darkness of frustration and sorrow, you can glean life's rarest treasures. If pain comes to you, see that it leaves something more than ugly scars. If some handicap visits you, don't lie down and lose the race—fight on and win spiritual victory. If trouble comes, don't simply shed tears. With God's help, turn your distress into a blessing.

Live in a Big World

We live where our thoughts are. If your thoughts are confined only to your business, only to your physical welfare, only to your narrow circle of friends, then you live a narrow and circumscribed life. But, if you are interested in what is going on in other parts of the world, if you read good books or listen to fine music then you live in a big world.

Ambition

In life we cannot always realize our ambition. Our plan is often upset and our dream is shattered. Few men are now doing what they first wanted to do. It takes courage to take a broken plan and make a great thing of it. Don't hold a grudge against life if you can't have your way. Take a second choice and make the best of it.

Loneliness

Everyone is subject to loneliness at times. What do you do in your lonely hours? Do you indulge in self-pity, and nurse your hurts and failures? Or do you bring God into your lonely hours and put him at your life's center? God will give you the power to stand up to life in your hours of loneliness.

Peace of Mind

No one can tell why some misfortune comes to us rather than to someone else. But, suppose we hold a grudge against life because it hurts us. We only injure others and ourselves. Our bitterness will infect our whole personality. It is better to drop our grudge and forgive everything and everybody. As soon as we do that, peace of mind will come to us.

Resentment

Many marriages are wrecked not by their wrongdoings but by resentment. A couple finds it hard going because some trait, some quality in one or the other or both, rubs the other the wrong way. This finally results in a festering sore. They must learn to overlook and forgive. Living together demands real skill.

How to Live

To seek God, the true and the beautiful; to master the art of being kind; to do our best under all circumstances; to think the best of others in spite of their faults; forgive and hold no grudges in the heart; to trust the ultimate decency of things and the love of God.

Finding Faults

If you seek to find faults in others, you will not be disappointed. You are sure to find them. But, if you go out to discover the good in men and women about you, you will find what a host of heroes and saints live in your homes and shops and streets. Look for the best instead of the worst.

Seeing Others Standpoint

All of us have difficulty getting along with certain people. They make us draw in on ourselves; it is hard to be outgoing and friendly with them. But, we try to understand them by asking the question, "Why do they act this way?" projecting ourselves into their situations and seeing life from their standpoint.

Live Every Day

"Here's hoping you will live every day of your life," wrote a friend. What he meant was he hoped his friend would live fully and happily every day. But do we really live or do we just last as long as we can? One life in all we have. We'd better not live a butterfly existence. We'd better live zestfully every day.

Your Life

Three factors combine to determine your life: heredity, environment and yourself. And the greatest of these is you. If you find nothing in life, invariably it is your own fault. Boredom and futility are the results, not of where you are or how much or how little you have, but of what you are. Life, even under circumstances over which you have no control, is largely what you make of it.

Just for Today

Just for today, I will try to live through this day only and not tackle my whole life's problems at once. Just today I will be happy. Just for today, I will try to strengthen my mind. I will study. I will not be a mental loafer. Just for today, I will adjust myself to what is, and not try to adjust everything to my own desires.

Good Prayer

Here is a good prayer: "Lord, keep me from the habit of thinking that I must say something on everything, on every occasion. Release me from the craving to straighten out other people's affairs. Keep my mind free from endless detail; give me wings to get to the point. Give me grace to listen to the recital of other's tribulations. Seal my lips against my own aches and pains."

Kindness

Someone said, "The joy of life is in its extras, the lovely things to do, the kind words we say, beyond what is expected of us." Yes, it is the unnecessary courtesies, the unexpected gifts, the uncalled for thoughtfulness and the surprises of kindness that make a happy home. It is the surplus goodness that makes us truly happy.

Age—State of Mind

Many people are unhappy because they have a fear of growing old. To them, even their birthdays become as occasion for grief. But, after all age is a state of mind. Our spirits need not grow old. What we should dead is the wrinkles of the mind, not the wrinkles of the body. A woman said, "I am 75 years young and it is wonderful to still be so young!"

Leadership

A good leader:
1. Sets good examples.
2. Gets results through other people.
3. Treats everyone as individuals.

4. Suggests or requests, rather than commands.
5. Asks questions before reprimanding; criticizes in private.
6. Leads rather than bosses.
7. Welcomes suggestions for improvement.
8. Praises good performance rather than criticizing the bad.

See Other People's Views

Most conflicts between parents and youngsters results from their inability to appreciate each other's point of view. As long as parents and children see a given situation only through their own eyes, disagreements are sure to follow. The clash between the two generations will come to an end if they learn to see things through each other's eyes.

Slow Down

Many a man acquires the notion that he must accumulate possessions by pushing and driving him to frenzy. In the process, he loses the ability to replenish his inner power. He has no time to sit down to relax or be silent. He has no time to take a daily walk or exercise. He loses his bodily strength and resistance. He dies prematurely.

Driving a Car Prayer

Here is a prayer for everyone who drives a car: "O God our Father, keep my hands steady, my eyes clear and my mind alert at all times. Forbid that my carelessness should harm another. Watch over me and anyone who may accompany me. Protect me from danger and from harm, and guide me safely to my journey end. Amen."

Accepting the Inevitable

An elderly man was always cheerful and content, although he had been up to his neck in trouble all his life. When asked the secret of his serenity, he replied, "I learned to cooperate with the inevitable." Certain things just can't be helped. They are beyond our control. Stop fighting difficulties that can't be avoided. Follow this man's philosophy. "Cooperate with the inevitable."

Forgive and Forget

No one can have peace of mind if he entertains resentment or grudges against others. Every person must forgive and forget the wrongs of others if he is to feel true serenity of soul. Feelings of antagonism and hatred become a great burden and excess baggage of the mind. Unless you can get rid of them, you will never experience peace of mind.

Think High

If you think you're outclassed, you are. You've got to think high to rise! You've got to be sure of yourself before you can ever win a prize. Life's battles don't always go to the stronger or faster man. But, sooner or later, the man who wins is the one who thinks he can.

Benefits to Exercise

Regular exercise like walking offers an excellent form of protection against circulation ailments such as arteriosclerosis, hardening of the blood vessel walls. Let us ride less and walk more. Physical fitness definitely has an important overall influence in a person's life. Not only does it help physically, but also mentally and spiritually.

Look at the Bright Side of Life

We all have the power of choice. We may choose to see our cup half empty, or half full. Today, let us see the bright side of life. Today, let us see what is right in our home, our work and our life. Today, let us see the good in our family and friends. Today, let us be thankful to God for all His blessings.

Mistake in Judging

Three blind men once touched an elephant. The first touched a leg and said, "It is like a tree." The second touched an ear and said, "It is like a leaf." The third touched the tail and said, "It is like a rope." All judged the elephant by part of it. In life, we often make the mistake of judging the whole by parts.

God's Gift

Radios with built-in alarm clocks were advertised with the words: "Begin the day with music." When the clock is set for a certain time in the morning, the sleeper is awakened by music from the radio. Why not begin the day with the music of a grateful heart thanking God for the gift of a new day?

Doing One Task at a Time

One of the causes of mental stress is the frustration that results from trying to do "everything at once." The remedy is to prepare a daily schedule of activities to be done. Tackle the most important first. Then, one after another finish each item on the list. Unfinished tasks induce tension, while finished ones promote relaxation.

Cure for Loneliness

Many people are overcome by loneliness, but it often is of their own making. As a remedy, we must be friends. Nine out of 10 times, loneliness comes because of our refusal to give ourselves away. Why not turn the key, open the door and forget yourself? You will be amazed to find how friendly the world is.

Love in Homes

There is sense of strain in many homes even though it does not break out in arguments. Blood relationship does not always mean love. It is a pity people take it for granted that it does. We forget to practice tenderness, consideration and tact, and as a result, love dies. We must always protect and care for the love that comes from our dear ones.

Pray Daily

Two men went fishing. A storm came up and it seemed their small boat would sink. One man began to pray. He said, "Lord, I have not asked you for anything for 15 years. If you will save us from this storm, I will not bother you again for another 15 years." Instead of making prayer a daily practice, some people use it only as an emergency measure in a crisis.

Forget Past Mistakes

It is better not to brood over a past mistake, no matter how serious it was. Admit your fault in the right spirit, then turn and face toward the light. Make the memory of it as incentive for better things. Our task is to transmute its evil into good.

Life's Possessions

We are pilgrims on earth. Our life here is brief—so brief as to merely an instant in the far reach of time. When we die, we cannot take with us all the possessions we accumulate in our short years. We don't even have the satisfaction, which the ancient Egyptians had, of having our hard possessions buried with us.

Living Life

Life has no bargain counters. In the long run, on life's road you get what you pay for, no more, no less. Of course, fortune and misfortune in any life depends entirely on what we do not come alike to all. But the final effect of fortune or misfortune in any life depends entirely on what we do with what comes to us. Even misfortune can be made to pay rich dividends when rightly used.

Life Adventures

Here is a list of five adventures:
1. Instead of going the old familiar road on your next trip, try a different route.
2. Pay a friendly call on a new acquaintance.
3. Read a good book about a subject new to you.
4. Show a personal interest in a boy or girl whose life may be influenced by an adult friend.
5. Take the responsibility of neighborhood leadership for something that needs to be done.

Life's Struggle

No matter who you are or how good you are, you cannot escape trouble. Struggle is part of every man's life. You must learn to face it. It may be that your trusted friend has betrayed you, or that you have failed in your business, or that death had taken away someone you love. Will you be defeated or victorious?

Life's Journey

In Albuquerque, New Mexico, there is a street named Shangri-la, a dead-end street. So many of the roads we start out on find Shangri-la turn out to be dead ends. The greatest mistake we make in life is to assume that somewhere there is a Shangri-la that will keep us happy with no further need for growth. Life must be a journey with more wonderful things always ahead.

Spiritual Victory

When life brings us a serious misfortune we tend to blame it on fate. We want to say, "Life is cruel to me. Fate is against me." But we do well to remember that whenever we are in trouble we are free to do something about it. With God's help we can make almost anything work. We can find a spiritual victory from our defeat.

Brighten Your Life

If you are unhappy, think of the most unfortunate person you know. As soon as you go to him and help him in some way, even if only with friendly word. It will not only encourage him but will set songs singing in your heart. You will experience real joy and the whole world will become brighter for you.

Unforgiving

Unforgiveness is like poison. No one can retain it without meeting disruption and pain. When there is unforgiveness in someone's heart, life is threatened. A family is disrupted and tension grows. Finally one's mental and physical health is impaired—all because forgiveness is not granted.

Kindness

Kindness is the finest of all arts in our unkind world. It is so simple that anyone can master. No one needs to be learned or famous to do a deed of kindness. All that is needed is a little thoughtfulness and considerateness of others. Every act of kindness is like a lighted candle in our dark and dismal world.

Aim High

If you believe anything at all, believe in yourself. Believe that you were born to succeed. Aim high. There is plenty of room at the top. It's the bottom that is crowded. Once your sights have been set on high ambitions proceed on course without faltering. Constantly keep the mental image of your aim before you as you go on toward its achievement.

Do Things Promptly

A man who had led a very busy life and made great accomplishments was asked, "How did you manage to do it all?" He replied, "The answer is simple. I did what I ought to do promptly." The trouble is we don't do what we ought to do promptly. We put it off by saying, "I'll get around to it someday." And that someday never comes.

Making a Mistake

There are two things we can do when we make mistakes. We can resolve that we will never make cowards of us. This is foolish. Or we can make up our minds that we will learn from our mistakes and so profit by the experience.

Success

Many people have a wrong idea about success. Success is not measured by the size of man's savings, nor kind of house he lives in, nor the power and price of the car he drives, but the kind of man he has made of himself and the contribution he is making to society. Success is not having, but giving himself.

Growing Old

The years bring their changes to us all. Age, ill health and handicaps bring us disappointments and frustrations. Some feel that they have been relegate to the junk is not so. If they open their eyes and see, they will find that they can still be useful. No one needs to be unhappy so long as he sees some use in the world.

Life Choices

Life is a compulsion—too long for some, too short for most. But if life itself is a compulsion, the manner of living is a choice. Life is what we make of it. Voltaire once described life as a bad joke. We can make life a joke, a game, a struggle, a quest, a conquest, a dreary lengthening-out of existence, a groveling in the mire or a flight toward the star we choose that matter in our lives.

Live One Day

If you want to live without worry, live one day at a time. Drop yesterday with its mistakes and failures. Shut out tomorrow with its foreboding. Each day is a little life. Don't waste your time with futile fears and morbid musings. Each day is a little life. Be glad and grateful for its wonder. Live it with confidence and joy.

Is God Dead?

One Sunday morning about church time a son asked his father, "Daddy, is God dead?" Yes, God is actually dead in many a home. There is no prayer, no church and no grace at the table. Burdened with a thousand and one activities, many parents leave out the most important thing in life—the spiritual nurture of themselves and their children.

All Kinds of People

While we live our short life on this earth, we come in contact with all kinds of people—people of various colors, shapes, sizes and ways of life. The problem is: What shall be the basis of our relationship with them? Some seek isolation. Some build a wall of prejudice. But life is deepest and richest when we seek to love and understand our neighbors.

Extras

"The joy of life is in its extras, the lovely things we do, the kind words we say, beyond what is expected of us." Yes, it is the unnecessary courtesies, the unexpected gifts, the uncalled for thoughtfulness and surprises of kindliness that make a happy home.

True Success

We often think of success in terms of money one has accumulated or fame one has attained. But here is a definition of true success: "He has achieved success who has lived well, laughed often and loved much; who has filled his niche and accomplished his task; who has always looked for the best in others and given the best he has."

Mud or Stars

"Two men looked out of the prison bars. One saw mud and the other stars." Life can be mud or stars depending on your outlook. If you have eyes only for criticism, you can always find fault in everything and everybody. On the other hand, if you have eyes of appreciation, lo, the whole world changes into one of beauty and loveliness.

An Understanding Parent

A parent's prayer: "O God, teach me to understand my children, to listen to them patiently and to answer all their questions honestly. Let me never nag; and when I am out of sorts, help me to hold my tongue. Let me praise them for all deserving deeds. May I encourage them to think, to choose and to make decisions. Make me an understanding parent."

Keeping Up with the Joneses

Many people lie awake at night worrying about how to make both ends meet. Rising prices and soaring taxes harass and annoy them. They try to stretch an income to obtain innumerable things they want. Stop keeping up with the Joneses. Learn to go without some luxuries. This is one way to live without worry.

Do It Now

If you intend to speak a kind word, speak it now. If you intend to do a kind deed, do it now. If you intend to write a letter to your friend, write it now. If you intend to send flowers to your loved one, send them today. Tomorrow may be too late. You may not be here tomorrow. Your friend or loved one may not be here tomorrow.

To Die is an Adventure

Life after death cannot be proved. But that ought not to disturb us. The things we can prove in life do not make life exciting. The most thrilling things are the uncertainties. To die is an adventure. Trust in God and do not fear death.

A High Opinion of Himself

A man was asked why he talked to himself so much. He replied, "For two reasons. First, I like to talk to a smart man. Second, I like to hear a smart man talk." This man had a high opinion of himself. There is something sacred in each one of us. Let us "be loyal to the royal" in ourselves.

Deadly Weapons

A food chemist once observed, "The deadliest weapons used by man on committing suicide are the knife, fork and spoon." We must keep our bodies fit by taking proper food, rest, exercise and sunshine. We must watch our weight. It is just as religious for us to observe the rules of good health as to pray to God to heal our sick bodies.

A Dagger

"If fate throws a dagger at you, there are two places to take hold of it—by the blade or by the handle." If fate throws a misfortune at you, you can take it by the blade of self-pity and it will cut and hurt you. If you take it by the handle, you can use it and turn it into a fortune.

The Sure Cure

High blood pressure, nervous breakdowns, ulcers and mental collapses are often caused, our doctors tell us, by negative thinking, evil imagination and confused emotions. It is hard to cure with pills, injections or surgery. The sure cure is the practice of love and forgiveness.

Right Where You Are

The most exciting and interesting place is right where you are. If the grass is greener in your neighbor's backyard, it usually is because he has made it greener. Stop envying others. You can make your life happier and better by changing your attitude. Do the best with what you have right where you are.

The Added Touch

The secret of success in any undertaking is the added touch—doing more than is expected. The store that gives the added service, the restaurant that serves the extra cup, the gasoline station that gives its customers superior service, the hotel that places a newspaper at each door in the morning—these have learned the secret of winning favor and business.

Stop Imaging Things

We often make ourselves miserable worrying about something that never happens. We make ourselves unhappy anticipating trouble that never comes. We spend agonizing hours expecting a malady from which we will never suffer. We lose sleep weeping over sorrows that never arrive. The best advice is: "Stop imagining things."

Human Beings

A child heard the term "human beings" but could not grasp its meaning. His mother explained, "It means all of us—father, mother, brother, sister, our neighbors, everyone we know is a human being." The child asked, "But all people we don't know, are they human beings?" Ah, there's the rub. All people we don't know, are they human beings too? Do we treat them as our brothers?

Only One Problem

In these days of pressure and tension, we are driven almost to distraction by our work. How many times have you thought as you went to bed, "How can I ever meet all the tasks of tomorrow?" But you must remember that in a given instant of time only one difficulty can possibly emerge to perplex you. You have to handle only one problem at a time.

Blue Days

Every person who reads this column will find he sometimes has dark days—days when he feels down in the dumps. So do I, and thousands of others, but we do well to remember that "blue days" do pass. We must not let them upset us and crush us. We must accept them, look upon them as passing clouds and wait until the sun shines—as it surely will.

The Same Dishes

A woman complained she washed the same dishes every day. If they were all stacked up, they would be higher than the Washington Monument. Yes, life is often colorless, deadly and monotonous. Every day we get up, eat, go to work, then come home and go to bed again. But, life is what we make of it. It depends on our attitude. Cheer up, friends. Pull yourselves together.

Frustration

Everywhere we meet men and women who are frustrated. To overcome the feeling of frustration we must accept facts about ourselves. One woman admitted, "The happiest day of my life was the day I gave up trying to be beautiful." There are some things you cannot do no matter how hard you try. To be happy, accept and be yourself.

How to Win Friends

A young woman asked her marital advisor how she could induce a certain young man to propose to her. The advisor replied, "The best way to get a husband is to talk to a man about himself." If you want to win friends, forget yourself and learn to love and be interested in other people. Practice the Golden Rule.

Never Trouble Trouble

There was a woman who for 50 years had the habit of looking under her bed every night for a burglar. If she found one she probably would have died of shock. Many people worry about things that never happen. Someone wisely said, "Better never trouble trouble until trouble troubles you."

The Way to Love

"The way to love anything is to realize it might be lost." As we mediate over it we will come to see its truth. A good way to love the members of our family is by remembering that they might be lost. A good way to love our country is by realizing that its blessings might be lost.

A Barrel of Gold

A kindly, happy man was once asked why he acted as though he didn't have a care in the world. He replied, "Because I have a barrel of gold at home." Some thieves broke into his home to steal his "barrel of gold." He did have a barrel of gold at home but no one could steal it. His barrel of gold was the love he had for his family, and the love his family had of him.

Never Say Die

A passenger was terribly seasick on the ship deck. A steward came along and said, "Cheer up, sir. No man ever died of seasickness." The sick man replied, "Please don't say that. It's the hope of dying that has kept me alive so far." No matter how discouraging a situation you may be in, never give up hope. Where there is life, there is hope.

Be Yourself

Some years ago Clark Gable took off his shirt in the movie *It Happened One Night* and showed that he wore no undershirt. This reduced that sale of men's underwear by 40 percent in a single year. It is pity people copy what others do. They think, talk, vote and live according to the social pattern. We need courage to be ourselves.

Our Turn

Almost every day we read of the death of someone we know. We are prompted to reflect, "Will my life be similarly cut short?" We all tend to think we have plenty of time and there is no hurry. But often "it is later than we think." We must do all the good we can before our turn comes.

Charity Begins at Home

The trouble with us is that we find it difficult to care for the people closest to us. We have not learned to love the very people whom we know the most. Charity begins at home. Let us be kind and affectionate ever mindful of our family and friends.

Identification

In introducing a speaker at a banquet once, the toastmaster had this to say about him: "This man has been closely identified with all good things in our community for more than 40 years." Identified with all the good things—what a tribute! A man's life is measured—not by his possessions—by things with which he has been associated and identified.

Sympathy

A man saw a number of children on a street, all crying. He asked them, "What's the matter with you children?" They answered, "We've all got a pain in Billy's stomach." Real sympathy is not simply feeling sorry for the misfortune of another. It is putting oneself in another's place. It is making somebody else's pain your own.

Giving is Receiving

A prosperous manufacturer donated to a church a pipe organ costing $25,000. Then the depression came and his business collapsed. Today he is on the caretaker's staff of the church to which he gave the organ. To a recent visitor he revealed his philosophy, "That which I kept, I lost, and that which I gave, I still have."

How to Die

A group of soldiers was being entertained before leaving for the warfront. One of them asked, "Will any of our friends here tell us how to die?" There was a silence. Then one of the singers began to sing the aria from "Elijah," "O Rest in the Lord." If we have a firm faith in God, we can face death without fear.

Be a Forgetter

Sometime ago a memory expert came to Honolulu to show people how to improve their memory. It is advantageous for us to have a good memory. But it is more important to be a good forgetter, provided we forget the right things. We do well to forget yesterday's neglects, failure, disappointments, sorrows, insults and grudges.

The Grumbling Habit

The worst habit to fall into is the grumbling habit. It can spoil the whole climate of one's life. To a grumbler nothing is right and something is the matter with everything. He sees only the gloomy side of life. A person who is occupied with complaints seldom thinks about the needs of others. He is constantly unhappy and dissatisfied.

Hunger for Appreciation

We all hunger for appreciation. We all crave the words of approval and recognition that our efforts seem worthwhile. It is tragic that many people keep on with their task, day in and day out, week in week out, and hardly anybody ever utters a word of praise for their efforts. Interest and encouragement are essential to life.

Being Neutral

A man described how he avoided getting involved in squabbles, "I just put myself in neutral and take it easy." The trouble with the world is that too many people have put themselves in neutral. They take no part in the struggle of right against evil. We must not be neutral in battles for civic decency, human rights, brotherhood and peace.

Life's Needs

Emerson said the needs of life are much fewer than most people realize. We need someone to love and be loved so that we can share our sorrows and our joys. We need something worth doing so that we can fill time and not kill it. We need faith in God that makes sense out of life.

Enlarging Our Circle

An old man used to repeat this prayer every day, "Lord, bless me and my wife, my son John and his wife, us four and no more." Some people are so self-centered that they don't care a bit about other people. We must broaden our outlook and include in our circle of concern other people. We must assume our responsibilities for or fellow human beings.

Real Education

Some people have the erroneous idea that education is cramming the mind of the child with facts and information. That is not so. The word "education" comes from the Latin verb *educare*, which means to draw out. Real education is drawing out the best in the child by the persuasive appeal of the teacher.

Only Once

The sudden death of a friend makes us realize that our life on this earth is short. We do well to think of the words of Phillip Brooks, "I expect to pass through this world but once; my good therefore that I can do, or any kindness I can show to any fellow creature, let me do it now. Let me not defer or neglect it, for I shall not pass this way again."

Meaningless Activity

A cartoon showed a husband and wife driving along a rapid pace on a desert road. The wife said, "I know we're lost, but I didn't want to say anything about it because we were making such good time." There are many people who keep themselves busy—and yet do nothing. The tragedy of life is meaningless activity without objective.

The Sound of Music

Shakespeare said, "The man who hath not music in his soul, who is not moved by concord of sweet sounds, is fit for treason's stratagems and spoils. Let no such man be trusted." Every human being should enjoy music. Music is a universal language which speaks its joy, its sadness or its challenge to all people everywhere.

Joining Our Hands

A little child was lost in a wheat field. His parents searched in vain to find the child. The neighbors and friends came to assist in the search. They couldn't find the child. Then someone suggested, "Why don't we join our hands and comb the entire field?" So they did. They found the child—dead. They said, "Why didn't we join hands sooner?"

Three More Years to Live

A man was told by his doctor that he had only three more years to live. Instead of brooding over his misfortune, he decided to spend the remaining three years of his life as best as he could. He read great books, listened to great music, visited orphanages and hospitals and did all he could for others. Just before he died, he said, "I have no regrets. I am ready to go."

God's Telephone Number

A preacher said, "The trouble is that we want to ring God up on the phone, but we don't know his number." Petty, selfish prayers will not reach God. If we have hate in our hearts, our prayers will die on our lips. God is known only through love. Love is the number. No other calls will reach him.

Criticism

In life we are bound to be misunderstood and criticized by others. Especially if you occupy a position of prominence you will certainly become the target of misunderstanding and abuses. Washington was called a hypocrite. Lincoln was described as original gorilla. Don't be upset by criticism. Do what is right in the sight of God and fear no one.

The Human Race

Confucianism says, "All within the four seas are brothers." Buddhism says, "There is no caste in blood which runneth of one hue." Christianity says, "God hath made of one blood all nations of men for to dwell on the face of the earth." Yes, at bottom, humanity is one. The human heart is everywhere the same with similar hopes, fears and aspirations. After all, whether we are black or white, yellow or brown, we belong to the same race: the human race.

We Live But Once

Yes, we live but once. We can't take with us the money we make or the worldly possessions we accumulate in this world when we die. The only thing we can take with us is the good we do in the world and kind deeds we do for others.

Be an Encourager

It you have anything encouraging to say, don't hold it back. Say it. The people around you need your encouragement. They may be starving for words of appreciation. Don't join the ranks of croakers and the grumblers. Be an encourager. Always be ready to praise, not condemn. See how many people you can lift and inspire during the day giving them words of encouragement.

Here is Today

Living in the past is folly. It is gone and will not come back. Living in the future is futile. We cannot tell what a day may bring forth. It will not be what we think, or fear or imagine it will be. In the meantime, here is today. It is all the time we need. If we use it right, with courage and kindness, it is enough. Here is today, good reader; your day, my day, our day. Let us live it—fully.

Life is a Boomerang

Life is a boomerang. What we do always come to us. We reap what we sow. An angry voice calls for an angry voice in return. A critical remark gets its reply in criticism. Quarreling breeds quarreling. Discontent breeds discontent. On the other hand, love begets love.

Thoughtfulness breeds thoughtfulness. Kindness gives birth to more kindness. Consideration and understanding creates a mutuality that makes meaningful relationships possible.

A Guilty Conscience

A man defrauded the government in making out his income tax return. He finally sent a letter to the Collector of Internal Revenue in which he wrote: "Enclosed you will find a check for $500. If I still can't sleep I'll send the balance of what I owe." In Nevada a man who had committed 30 years previously gave himself up to the law saying, "My conscience has bothered me so long I can't stand it any longer." No one can have peace of mind if he has a guilty conscience.

We Wear Masks

We all wear masks—masks intended to hide our loneliness, fears, hopes and misgivings. Sometimes we wear masks intended to deceive others into thinking more highly of us than we deserve. We wear masks at times to deceive even ourselves. It is important that we know our real self, and really and honestly understand ourselves with masks removed. We need to know, understand and accept our deep lying motives and desires.

Success is a Journey

Someone said, "Success is a journey, not a destination." Success lies in the effort, satisfaction and happiness you derive as you struggle to reach a goal. If you reach your goal, you must set up another goal if you want to make your life zestful. Success is to feel that life is good despite all its trials and troubles. Life stagnates when you feel you have no more goals to strive for.

Loss of Your Loved One

Have you lost your dearest one and you feel depressed and lonely? Then do not spend all your time on the blessed memories of the past and live a closed life. Open your life to new friendships and new interests. Find something to keep you actively engaged. Find someone or some interest to even partially replace the emptiness the loss of your loved one has created. I am sure this is what your loved one would want you to do.

Learn to Laugh

A sense of humor is a saving grace. A bad-tempered person doesn't enjoy life. He takes himself too seriously. He doesn't see the funny side of life. He never looks in a mirror and laughs at himself. An old preacher said, "If you could just sit on the fence and see yourself pass, you die laughing at the sight." There are so many things in life that makes us pessimistic and sad. Why not cultivate a sense of humor. Let's learn to laugh—often.

He Gave Up Praying

A little boy had long prayed for a baby brother. But no baby brother came. He gave up praying. One morning his dad took him to his mother's room, where twin brothers awaited his inspection. He said, "Gee, Dad, isn't it lucky I stopped praying when I did?" God doesn't give us everything we ask for, for some things we ask for are not good for us.

Express Praise and Appreciation

A wife lamented, "My husband and I have been married 24 years and if he ever told me I looked nice, or that a meal was good, I'd die of shock." Husband and wife must cultivate the art of expressing praise and appreciation. They shouldn't have to search far to find something to praise in each other. No one is perfect. Overlook the faults in the other and see only the good. Learn to express sincere praise and appreciation.

TLC

A hospital nurse talking to a friend kept referring to a TLC patient. Puzzled, her friend asked what she meant by a TLC patient and the nurse explained, "That's what they write on the chart when the doctors won't know what else can be done for a patient. He is to get TLC—tender loving care." What every patient needs is tender loving care. In fact, to live a normal, healthy life everyone needs TLC.

I am Sorry

The three magic words that can restore broken relationships are "I am sorry." No dispute can be settled if each side insists on putting the entire blame on the other. When one side says, "The fault was mine, I am sorry," the other side is bound to say, "I was at fault, too." It takes a lot of courage to admit one's fault. Let us learn to say the three magic words.

Greatness

Greatness lies in living for things that last. Here is a teacher who teaches her children in the faith she is molding lives. Here is a politician who makes speeches not merely to get votes but because he desires a better community. Here is an artist who writes a poem or carves a statue that will outlast his life. Here is a man who espouses a cause because he is anxious to bring about a better and more brotherly world.

Retirement

Many people long for the time when they may be relieved of all responsibility. They think retirement will be the solution to all their problems. If they can get out from under the load of life, they think they can live a happy state forever. But life of constant relaxation would be just another name for hell. A man who retired comparably young with an adequate income said, "I must find something to do. I am getting tired of just playing golf."

Give to the Living

An array of beautiful flowers is usually seen at a funeral service. Have you thought of the joy and happiness those flowers might have brought to the deceased if they had been given while he was alive? If you have flowers to give, give them to the living. If you have kindness to show, show it while your friend is still alive.

A Duck's Back

A wise man said, "We must have a sense of humor and a duck's back—let irritations run off like water from the back of a duck." Yes, we do well to laugh off slights, insults and irritations. If we don't they stick like thorns in our mind and hurt us. When told that Stanton had called him a fool, Lincoln said, "Stanton is usually right. If he says I am fool, I must be one." Saying this, he burst out laughing. Let us have a duck's back.

Body is the Temple of God

It is our duty to keep ourselves physically fit. Eating properly, sleeping well and taking exercise are not outside the province of religion. They are as much a part of religion as prayer and worship. A healthy, strong body is essential to the fullest kind of life. A Japanese proverb says, "A sound mind resides in a sound body." Let us remember our body is "the temple of God" and take excellent care of it.

Real Success

Many people are deluded into thinking they are succeeding when their business is growing, when their bank deposits are piling, when their securities are paying more dividends, when their golf score is improving, and when they are members of exclusive clubs. They are often "rich in things but poor in soul." Real success lies in possession of character, not of things.

Feeling Important

All human beings have one thing in common—a need to feel important. Everyone craves to be looked up to, to be somebody. None of us enjoy being treated like a push button or payroll number. If you have people working under you, build your workers' self-esteem by letting them know how much you appreciate their help. Treat them as human beings.

Wedlock or Deadlock?

Life is like marriage. How beautiful love begins. It starts with a fine romance. When a young couple is married how happy they look. They have qualities that can start a happy home. But the question is: "Have they the steady abiding love that keeps a home?" A wedding can result in a happy wedlock or a miserable deadlock. A good beginning is not enough. You need the power to see it through.

Not Sorry for 10 Things

Here are 10 things for which no one has been sorry:
1. For doing good to all.
2. For speaking no evil of no one.
3. For hearing before judging.
4. For thinking before speaking.
5. For holding an angry tongue.
6. For being kind.
7. For asking pardon for all wrongs.
8. For being patient toward everybody.
9. For praising others.
10. For disbelieving evil reports.

Running Away from Life

Our world is full of fleeing people who are unconsciously running out on life. They are running away from the difficulties, drudgeries and even the realities of life. To escape they resort to drugs, alcohol and all sorts of artificial stimuli. To avoid a problem or a difficulty they run for shelter, take wings to the world of make believe. There are thousands of suicides yearly, and suicide is really running away.

Real Riches are Within

We may not have so much of wealth, but we are rich indeed if we have health. We are rich indeed if we have eyes to see the beauty of trees and the glory of flowers. We may not be able to travel far, but joy is ours if we can hear songs of birds and laughter of children. We are rich indeed if we have the spirit of gratitude and are thankful for each day, come weal, come woe. After all, real riches are within us.

An Age of Speed

We are living in the age of speed. A generation ago, a man could travel as fast as a horse could carry him. Then came the automobile and the speed of travel was increased many times. Then came the airplanes and men were flying hundreds of miles an hour. Now the jet plane can travel faster than the speed of sound. But the question is, "Do we know where we are going?"

The Second Best

A young man working in a hospital laboratory had hoped to become a doctor but due to financial problems had to give it up. Now he was going to become a laboratory technician. The world is full of people who dream of great accomplishment but, due to various reasons, cannot realize them. For the problem is to adjust to the second best and make it successful.

Kindness and Courage

On the chimney of an old farmhouse in New England these lines were written: "Two things stand in stone—kindness in another's troubles and courage in one's own." Everyone can practice those "two things that stand like stone." We can show kindness to others in trouble and show courage in accepting and overcoming our own troubles.

Hating Our Enemies

When we hate our enemies, we are in a way giving them power over us. We don't sleep well. We lose our appetites. Our blood pressure goes up. Our health is impaired and we become unhappy. Our enemies would rejoice if they knew how they were making us suffer. Our hate is not hurting them at all. But it is turning our own days and nights into a hellish turmoil.

Self-Pity

Do you feel sorry for yourself? Beware of indulging in self-pity. Perhaps coveted honors have not come your way, or your pet plans have been thwarted or you are disappointed in life or in love. Don't go around with a "chip on your shoulder" feeling you are not appreciated. After all, disappointments, problems, handicaps and other obstacles are part of life and rightly handled, actually can become stepping stones to better things.

Incentives to Living

Sometime ago a young woman stenographer climbed out on the narrow edge of a high building and, while a crowd watched, jumped to her death. For an hour a minister and three policemen had pleaded with her not to take her life. Suppose you had been there with that girl—what would you have said to her? Good reader, what are to you the incentives to living?

Television Screen

Nowadays we don't entertain ourselves; we have to be entertained. We have a pitifully small stock of interests and ideas. We read fewer and fewer books and look at more and more television. Conversation is becoming a lost art because for nights on end families sit in silence, their eyes riveted on a television screen. We have more leisure than ever before but we fritter away time aimlessly and trivially.

True Friends

It is easy to make fair weather friends who flock to you when prosperity is your position. In adversity the line of friendship becomes thin. When your prestige slackens or your money fails, then so-called friends will drop away like leaves from a tree in autumn. You are fortunate if you have friends who stand by you through thick and thin.

Take Time

"Take time to think—it is a source of power. Take time to play—it is the secret of perennial youth. Taker time to read—it is the source of wisdom. Take time to love—loving is what makes living worthwhile. Take time to be friendly—friendships give life a delicious flavor. Take time to laugh—it is the music of the soul. Take time to give—any day of the year is too short for selfishness. Take time to show appreciation—thanks is the frosting on the cake of life."

You Are Not Old If

Here is a thought-provoking poem: "Age is a quality of mind. If you have left your dreams behind, if hope is lost, if you no longer look ahead, if your ambition's fires are dead, then you are old. But, if from life, you take the best and keep the jest; if love you hold, no matter how the years go by, no matter how the birthdays fly, you are not old."

Off Days

All of us have off days, when we get out of bed on the wrong side, and everything goes wrong all day long. A woman said to her husband, who had for the first time brought home a bouquet of flowers, "Everything has gone wrong—the washing machine broke down, Johnny fell off his bicycle and got hurt, I dropped a vase and broke it and now you come home drunk!" If we have an off day, it is better to take a day off to get things right.

When a Loved One Dies

There comes a time in everyone's life when a loved friend or relative passes away. We miss the person. And the thought that nothing in heaven or earth can bring the person back burdens us with grief and hopelessness. But when we think that we had no "lease" on his personality—no right to keep him for our sake—the thought begins to creep into our heart that we ought to be glad for the time we had him. Instead of grief there should be gratitude.

A Purpose in Life

Life becomes zestful when one has a purpose. The mother in the home, trying to make both ends meet; the teacher in the school, working with difficult children; the businessman at his work, doing his best to keep his business going; the student in school, struggling to get an education—all these make life meaningful because they have a purpose.

How to Live Longer

How to live longer: Eat less, chew more. Worry less, work more. Hurry less, read more. Smoke less, breathe more. Grumble less, praise more. Hate less, love more. Talk less, think more. Ride less, walk more. Waste less, give more. Preach less, practice more. Bray less, pray more. Rush less, relax more.

Sin of Procrastination

We often commit the sin of procrastination. We say to ourselves that someday we are going to send flowers to our neglected friends. But we end up be sending them to the funeral parlor. We intend to write a letter to someone. But we end up be sending a letter of condolence to the bereaved family. We say to ourselves that someday we are going to tell someone how much we love him. But we end up by putting the sentiment on the tombstone.

A Row of Coffins

A young soldier stood before a row of coffins containing the bodies of his father, mother and six brothers and sisters, all killed in a railroad accident. Their last letters to the homesick soldier serving overseas told of the welcome they were planning for him when he came home. What can one cling to in an hour like that? If you haven't God, what have you?

How a Child Learns

If a child lives with criticism, he learns to condemn. If a child lives with hostility, he learns to fight. If a child lives with fear, he learns to be apprehensive. If a child lives with encouragement, he learns to be confident. If a child lives with praise, he learns to appreciate. If a child lives with security, he learns to have faith in himself.

Give Me a Good Digestion

This prayer hangs on the wall of a church: "Give me a good digestion, Lord, and also something to digest. Give me a healthy body, Lord, with sense to keep it at its best. Give me a healthy mind, good Lord, to keep the good and pure in sight. Give me a mind that is not bored, that does not whimper, whine or sign. Give me the grace to see a joke."

On a Suicide Bridge

A blind man was lost on a bridge at night. A feminine voice asked him, "Are you having trouble?" The blind man replied, "I seem to be lost." Getting his address the young woman escorted him home. The blind man thanked her profusely. The woman said, "I should thank you instead. I was on the bridge to commit suicide. Now I am not going to. Good night."

Forgiveness

Forgiveness is essential to our health of mind and body. Friendships are often marred or ruined by lack of forgiveness. Misunderstanding and ill-feeling exist between people when a little frank talk and forgiveness can mean peace and happiness. Family rifts exist for years when forgiveness could restore harmony and happy unity. To forgive is to live.

Mastery of Skill

Paderewski, famed pianist, said that if he left off practice for one day he could tell the difference. If he left it off for two days his friends could tell the difference. If he left it off for three days his audience could tell the difference. The mastery of any skill is achieved only through stern discipline and laborious training.

Where Trouble Comes

There are three ways people react when they face trouble. Some go off by themselves and brood. This is bad. Some dash around to tell the neighbors about it. This is better. He will not face a breakdown but the neighbors may. The third reaction is the most wholesome—get busy and do something.

How to Find Happiness

A young man wrote, "You talk of happiness, but I have never found it." You can never find happiness if your thoughts are self-centered. You can find it when you go to unhappy places and make people happy. You can find it when you fill up the emptiness of people, when you show your love and concern for the unfortunate. You can find it when you see the happy faces of others and realize you have caused their happiness.

Final Questions

When you and I have finished our work on earth and moved to our reward, we will not be remembered chiefly for the positions we held or the money we accumulated. Rather we will be remembered for what we accomplished in terms of service to our fellow men and the spirit in which we performed our duties. We will not be asked, "How much money did you accumulate?" or "What position did you hold?" but "How much good did you do for your fellow human beings?"

In Spite of It

A woman despaired, "I have so much trouble, I wish I were dead." A man cried out, "Trouble after trouble has come upon me, I can't take it anymore." It is not a question of whether trouble will come. No one is immune to it. It will do little good to ask why it comes. The one question upon which hangs your health, your happiness and your usefulness is "How can I face it and live triumphantly in spite of it?"

Life is What We Make It

A man said on his 80th birthday, "If I could have my way I would like to live every day of these years all over again." A girl jumped from a hotel window, leaving this note: "I am 21 years old, I have seen all there is of life. It is a nightmare. I cannot stand any more of it. Goodbye." Whether life is ecstasy or a nightmare depends on one's attitude. Life is what we make it.

A Thick Skin

We often say of a person, "He has a thick skin." It means he is an insensitive person, indifferent to the feelings of others. How thick is your skin? Do you have a skin like that of a hippopotamus? If you go through life with thick skin and a blunted heart, you will be shut out from life's adventures in human relationships. You must sharpen your sensitivity and imagination so that the hurts and sorrows of others will become your own.

Going Two Miles

The world is full of half-successful people. They are those who miss being great because they do their duty and no more. They are the ones who keep their eyes on the clock and scrupulously do what is required of them, but no more. To be truly successful you must go beyond the frontier of duty and requirement. Asked to go one mile, you must be willing to go two miles. You must put forth the extra effort. You must go beyond the call of duty.

The True Teacher

Paying tribute to his teacher, a young man said, "He has passionate desire to put in each student's hand a candle of discovery." The task of a teacher is not merely to transit information from textbook to notebook, but to awaken the interest of his students so they will find joy in discovering things or themselves. The true teacher helps his students to do his own thinking, to make his own discoveries and to develop his own mental capacities.

End of Your Rope

Someone said, "If you come to the end of your rope you must tie a knot and hang on." It is said the difference between cowardice and courage is the ability to hold on five minutes longer. Is some situation discouraging to you? Are you facing the dark night of affliction? Do you feel trapped with no way out of your difficulty? Don't lose heart. Don't give up. Look up to God for help with his strength hang on. A way will soon open for you.

Get Away from Civilization

The beauty in nature has an invigorating, cleansing quality. Damage caused by the stress and strain of modern life can be repaired when in contact with mother earth. It is not good for man's spirit always to walk on concrete and be jostled by harassed multitudes, or listen to the roar of traffic and breathe polluted air. We must get away occasionally from our busy round of duties and find release sitting under green trees in the mountains or sunning our bodies on the beach.

Definition of Success

He has achieved success who has lived well, laughed often and loved much; who has gained the respect of intelligent men and the love of little children; who has filled his niche and accomplished his task; who leaves the world better than he found it whether by a perfect poem or a rescued soul; who has never lacked appreciation of earth's beauty, or failed to express it; who has always looked for the best in others and given the best he had; whose life was an inspiration and whose memory a benediction.

The Human Race

There are four blood types of blood—A, B, AB and O. All are found in all races. Someone said "Biology and the Bible agree that God has made of one blood all nations of men." We must look upon all people, whatever the color of their skin, as our brothers and sisters, as members of our human family. After all, there is only one race: the human race.

Man and the Immense Universe

Recently two astronomers in Cambridge, Massachusetts discovered the largest structure ever seen in the universe: a collection of galaxies forming a sheet of least 500 million light years long. The immensity of the universe staggers our imagination. But let us remember that the shining eyes of man behind the telescope are more wonderful and significant than the immense universe which the telescope reveals.

Life's Attitude

A man grouses, "For every ounce of pleasure in this lousy life, there is a pound of pain. For every good person, there are a thousand scoundrels. Life is cruel and unjust." Yes, life can be cruel and rotten and unjust, but it can also be interesting and exciting and joyous, depending on our attitude. Life is 90 percent attitude.

Nothing to Retire To

The number of people who are retiring is growing. Someone made this observation: "The trouble with most people is that they have enough to retire on, but nothing to retire to." It is an erroneous notion that if you have enough money you will be happy. Wealth alone will not contribute to the richness of one's life. It is not enough to have money to live on. You must have something to live for.

A Child's Bill of Rights

Here are five articles in A Child's Bill of Rights:
1. His right to have his confidence kept when he has given it in faith.
2. His right to have questions and opinions treated seriously.
3. His right to a promise being kept.
4. His right to a share in family joys and sorrows.
5. His right to firm guidance in matters he is too inexperienced to figure out himself.

You Ain't Got It

A man was seeing the West for the first time, traveling by bus. He was not only unimpressed, but sharply critical of such wonders as the Grand Canyon, the Royal Gorge and the Painted Desert. The bus driver said to the disgruntled tourist, "Listen, mister, if you ain't got it on the inside, you can't see it on the outside." What we see depends on what we are inside.

What is Success?

What is success? To some, the accumulation of money will mean success. Others, success will mean bringing up good, happy and healthy children. To still others, serving humanity by becoming a teacher, doctor minister or social worker will mean success. Money is never the yardstick of success. Some have millions of dollars, but are bankrupt in character.

Blowing Your Top

Do you get angry often? Do you blow your top over small matters? Remember, when you get angry, you are actually hurting yourself.

Your sleep, your appetite, your blood pressure and your health are affected. Even your looks become harden. In anger you cannot think straight. An angry person cannot find peace of mind. So as in Hawaii we say, "No huhu!" (Don't get angry).

Cultivate Good Music

Music can bring enlargement of mind and heart. It uplifts us and carries us out of ourselves. It brings our souls out of the narrow confines of routines. It transports us from our mundane world to an enchanted one of beautiful sounds. It behooves all of us to cultivate good music and enrich our starving souls.

A Modern Tragedy

Nowadays the family is seldom together. Fewer and fewer are the quiet evenings spent by the entire family. Each member goes his own way. Each lives in his own world, pursuing his own interests. The family seldom united, except at a wedding or a funeral. The modern home is becoming a dormitory and a restaurant, a place to sleep and eat at all hours. There is little time to chat and share life together. This is a modern tragedy.

Take Time to Play

It is tragic that many people forget to play. A couple getting started with their home and family have to work hard. But the trouble is they forget to stop "getting started." A young man works hard to get good things for his family, but in doing so often loses his family. Take time out from your busy hours. Play with your family.

Literally a Change of Heart

After recovering from a heart attack that kept him bedridden for six months, a businessman said, "Isn't it funny that one must collapse with a serious disease before he learns how to live? Look at me—the worry wrinkles are gone, no more burning the candle at both ends. I've had six months to think what is and what is not important."

Laughter is the Best Medicine

Scientists studying the effects of laughter on human beings have found, among other things, that laughter has an immediate beneficial effect on virtually every important organ in the human body. It reduces health-sapping tensions, relaxes the tissues and exercises the most vital organs. Laughter is the best medicine for a long and happy life. He who laughs, lasts.

A Good Conversationalist

"A gossip is one who talks to you about others. A bore is one who talks to you about himself. A brilliant conversationalist is one who talks to you about yourself." If you aspire to become a good conversationalist, learn to be an attentive listener. Concentrate your attention on what the other person has to say to you. Talk less, listen more.

Lessons in Living

A credo on living:
1. Learn to laugh. A merry heart is better than medicine.
2. Learn to say kind things. Nobody ever resents them.
3. Learn to stop grumbling. Try to see good in the world.
4. Learn to relax. Many people get sick being always on the go.
5. Above all, learn to smile. It helps brighten the world.

Where is Happiness?

Our happiness comes from simple things like love and friendship, a clear conscience, a peaceful mind, a gentle and kindly spirit, a sense of duty and an awareness of beauty. Happiness does not depend on the position we hold, the size of our bank account, or whether we live in one room or a mansion. As someone said, "Happiness is an inside job."

When Their Daughter Died

A couple seemed unable to overcome their grief when their seven-year-old girl died. So many things around the house reminded them of her—her room, her playthings, the vacant chair at the table. Later, the husband said, "Instead of thinking of what we have lost, let's begin to think of what we have possessed. We have had seven years of joy from Mary's life, and nothing that has happened can take that away."

A Wedding or a Funeral?

A minister was asked which he preferred: officiating at a wedding or a funeral. He replied, "Funeral. Then I know their troubles are over." Unfortunately, too often marriage becomes the beginning of trouble. Glamour soon wears off and tensions rise over differences of temperaments and opinions. Marriage can succeed only when husband and wife develop a mutual sense of sharing and consideration.

A Delinquent Child

Here are five ways to make your child a delinquent:
1. Don't give him religious or spiritual training.
2. Don't let him discuss his plans or problems so he will not develop affection, security or trust in you.
3. Don't be concerned where he spends his free time.
4. Never praise him for his worthwhile efforts.
5. Just don't pay attention to what he does.

You Make Your Own Face

Life's struggles even affect and change the features of our faces. In a sense, everybody makes his or her face. Lincoln's face, so homely in its features, was an inspiration to millions because its lines and wrinkles represented the tenderness and strength of a great soul which had triumphed in life's struggles. After all, your face is your own, upon it are written your life's experiences.

Average or Excellent

A student in medical school was lazy. He was called into the office of the dean who criticized him for his poor scholarship. The student protested, "Well, I'm doing average work, am I not?" "Yes," said the dean, "but do you want to be an average doctor?" If anyone wants to excel in his profession, he must put forth his best efforts.

The Easiest Exercise

There is no excuse for anyone not taking daily exercise. The easiest is walking. Walking can be fun if you know how to make it so. Why not walk a couple of blocks and see how many new things you can discover while doing so. You will probably be surprised to see the number of things that had escaped your notice.

A Lighted Candle

Kindness is the finest of all arts in our unkind world. It is so simple anyone can master it. No one need be learned or famous to do a deed of kindness. All that is needed is a little thoughtfulness and consideration of others. Every act of kindness is like a lighted candle in our dark and dismal world.

Escape From Problems

A minister met his friend George on the street. Seeing that he seemed depressed, he asked him, "What's the matter, George?" He answered, "It's these problems. Nothing but problems and more problems." The minister said, "I was recently in a place where there were more than 100,000 people and not a single person had a problem." George suggested, "That's the place for me." The minister replied, "Woodlawn Cemetery in Bronx. All are resting in peace."

As the Doctor Orders

A doctor gives us this prescription:
1. Don't keep a killing pace of life.
2. Get down to normal weight and eat a well-balanced diet.
3. Develop the proper balance between work, play and sleep.
4. Take mild exercise daily.
5. Have a hobby or two.
6. Do things for others.
7. Have an occasional checkup.

Here's to Long Life

A health expert offers these tips that can help you live a long life:
1. Eat a balanced diet, consisting of lean meat, raw fruit and vegetables.

2. Whenever possible, eat fish and fowl.
3. Go easy on salt.
4. Avoid caffeine-filled beverages.
5. Drink eight glasses of water daily.
6. Weigh yourself often.
7. Eat slowly.
8. Learn to relax and rest.
9. Avoid smoking.
10. Don't worry.

Eros and Agape

It is said there are two kinds of love. One is *eros*, the popular idea of love. A person loves another only because of the attractiveness of the person or satisfaction the other person brings—in a social, economic or sexual way. The other is *agape*, the love that exists for the other person and seeks only happiness of the other person.

Troubles Caused By Yourself

Most of your problems and failures are caused by one person—yourself. You try to put the blame on circumstances, your friends, your wife or husband. But, if you are honest with yourself, you must admit that you are the cause of most of your troubles.

Learn What Life Is

Life cannot be measured by its length. Few would say he who lives longest lives the best. It is possible for a man who has lived long to have lived little. The value of a painting is not decided by the size of the canvas. The worth of life is not determined by its length. It is not how long or how short we live counts, but how deeply.

Commandments for Parents

1. You will break no promises.
2. You will not be over protective, but allow your child to learn from his own mistakes.
3. You will teach your child by example, as well as by precepts.
4. You will instill no fears in your child.

5. You will try to earn his love by being fair, with humor and understanding.
6. You will not force your child to develop into your own image, but allow him to become the best person his own nature permits.

Eyes to See Beauty

One may walk along a road and see beautiful trees and flowers or gaze upon majestic mountains without noticing them. One may look upon the beautiful Hawaiian sunset without commenting on it. Some may view a beautiful painting and see just a lot of paint spread carelessly on a piece of canvas. Our eyes, the windows of our souls, must be trained to see the wonders of nature and the works of art.

Life's Most Important Lesson

The most important lesson we must learn in life is to live in peace with others. If we are tempted to speak a sharp word, let us check it. If we find ourselves becoming intolerable, let us suppress it. If there is a temptation to be argumentative, let us shun it. If we feel inclined to show an unloving attitude, let us change it.

Everyday Dictators

We find dictators everywhere. Here is a father who dominates his family. Here is a mother who insists on living the lives of her children in detail. Here is an in-law who tries to boss everything. Here is a child who gets his own way by having tantrums. The dictators make life miserable in the home, in the club or even in the church.

Winning People to You

Here are six rules for winning people to your side:
1. Treat everyone you meet as though he or she is important.
2. Be friends.
3. Let the other person do the talking. Be a good listener.
4. Don't argue. You may win a point, but you will lose a friend.
5. Put yourself in the person's shoes.
6. Practice finding good in others. ✺